UPPER MERION TOWNSHIP
Library

Presented by

The American Association

of

University Women

2008

12 Going on 29

12 Going on 29

SURVIVING YOUR DAUGHTER'S TWEEN YEARS

Silvana Clark and Sondra Clark

PRAEGER

Westport, Connecticut
London

Library of Congress Cataloging-in-Publication Data

Clark, Silvana.
    12 going on 29 : surviving your daughter's tween years / Silvana Clark and Sondra Clark.
        p. cm.
    Includes bibliographical references and index.
    ISBN 978-0-275-99416-7 (alk. paper)
    1. Preteens. 2. Mothers and daughters. 3. Parent and child. I. Clark, Sondra. II. Title.
III. Title: Twelve going on twenty-nine.
HQ777.15.C53 2007
649′.133—dc22   2007022783

British Library Cataloguing in Publication Data is available.

Library of Congress Catalog Card Number: 2007022783
ISBN: 978-0-275-99416-7

First published in 2007

Praeger Publishers, 88 Post Road West, Westport, CT 06881
An imprint of Greenwood Publishing Group, Inc.
www.praeger.com

Printed in the United States of America

The paper used in this book complies with the
Permanent Paper Standard issued by the National
Information Standards Organization (Z39.48–1984).

10 9 8 7 6 5 4 3 2 1

Contents

Introduction

Remember all the advice well-meaning friends gave you when you were pregnant? You heard graphic descriptions on the pain of childbirth and what it's like to be sleep deprived with a colicky baby that introduces you to projectile vomiting.

You survived.

Later, friends shared the trials of living through the Terrible Twos with toddlers who refuse to take no for an answer as they pound an older sibling's violin against a window.

You survived.

A few years later, books and magazines gave cautionary advice on helping your 5-year-old adjust to school and the beginning of peer pressure.

You survived.

Now friends, books, magazines, and your mother are warning you about the Terrible Tweens. This stage, according to the TV experts, is where your normally cheerful 10-year-old shaves her head, pierces body parts you can't see, and goes drinking with members of her motorcycle riding gang.

You'll survive.

Yes, you'll survive because the majority of tweens are still girls who collect stuffed animals and occasionally snuggle next to you while reading the Sunday comics.

The past 10 years have seen an increase in marketers reaching the tween market. Back in the 1980s when I ran camps and recreational programs for children, we had three basic age groups: preschoolers were 3- to 5-year-olds, followed by children ages 6–12, and then the teen programs for ages 13 and above. Now tweens make up a subgroup—and a controversial subgroup at that. *Newsweek*, running a cover story on tweens, defined them as children between the ages of 8 and 13. Another magazine proclaimed that tweens are the 6- to 13-year-olds. (What happened to "children"?) In defining tweens for this book, we'll stick to girls between the ages of 9 and 13. These girls are too old for Barbies, but not old enough to date and read *Cosmo*.

In speaking to mothers across the country, one point is very clear: Moms feel their daughters are growing up too fast. Girls hear provocative lyrics in songs without fully understanding what the words mean. Fashion magazines encourage outfits that many mothers put in the category of "pre-prostitute." Schools offer sex education classes beyond the developmental ability of your 9-year-old daughter.

This book capitalizes on what most moms know in their hearts—that their tween daughter is still a child, still wanting to play silly games and bake cookies with them on a rainy Saturday afternoon. As a former camp counselor, I have memories of many 12- and 13-year-old girls arriving at camp with their pseudosophisticated attitude. Many had French manicures to accent their perfectly highlighted hair. Craft classes? How childish! Carry a backpack on an overnight hike? No way! Where would they plug in their hair dryer? But fast-forward two days and suddenly those tweens, away from cell phones and computers, are planning how to win the fort-building competition using tree limbs. They're proudly displaying the basket they wove in craft class. Those tweens find themselves excited about "shaving" a shaving cream–covered balloon. They giggle hysterically while making up a song about dirty socks. In other words, their pseudosophistication disappears as they engage in age-appropriate activities.

We can't shield our daughters from everyday life with its sex-infused commercials and peer pressure to dance like celebrities on MTV. We can, however, provide opportunities for them to engage in educational, fun, and wholesome activities that will give them a positive self-image. This book looks at the positive side of raising your tween daughter. We'll all face difficult situations that have us doubting our parenting capabilities. Yet, as you read comments from other mothers in this book, you'll see that *parent* is also a verb. By taking action and guiding your daughter into her teen years, you'll have an above-average chance she won't be riding off on her motorcycle, bald, with her tattooed head shining in the sun.

To get another opinion on raising tweens, you'll read comments from an expert… an expert in that she recently came through the tween years herself with creativity, chutzpah, and great fashion sense. My 17-year-old daughter Sondra, herself the author of six books, shares her thoughts about what it's like to be a tween. Let's face it, our memories can't recall all the details from those days when we were gangly 11-year-olds terrified at having to take showers in gym class. You'll also read comments from numerous other tweens and their moms, as they share thoughts and questions on a survey.

The mother of a tween is like a root beer float. First of all, root beer floats evoke the image of fun, of being together with friends or celebrating a happy occasion. Let's never forget that tweens are fun! You represent the ice cream, the substance of the drink. Then along comes your tween daughter in the form of root beer. It's a balancing act as you pour just enough root beer in the glass before it hits the ice cream and fizzes over. You and your daughter have a balancing act also. She wants independence; you want to protect her. She wants to post on MySpace; you want her to keep reading Little House on the Prairie books. Sometimes a balance works out between you and your daughter in the same way the root beer and ice cream balance out to make a great drink. And that foam that rises on top of the glass? That's the extra fun you get from being around a girl who is developing into a young woman!

This book gives practical ideas on how to make the mother-tween daughter relationship an enriching and positive experience. But wait! There's more! You'll also get fun ideas on how to have a SPARKS party with your daughter, reenact William Tell shooting an arrow through the apple on his son's head, develop a Funny List, make a wall hanging from old CDs, learn how to bake ribbon to make curly hair clips, and understand why it's important to take your daughter to watch a student protest at your local college. See how great it is to have a tween daughter?

Chapter 1

She's Smart—So Why Is School So Hard?

Is this a typical week at your house?

Monday: Your daughter comes home from school with a glowing report. "I love school! Lindsey and I get to start a school newspaper and we get to write articles and draw pictures and my name is going to be on the cover and we'll miss science because we have a special newspaper meeting and . . ."

Tuesday: Your daughter comes home from school and says, "School sucks! Why do I always get picked last in PE? I'm not that bad at softball, but no one wants me on their team. I'm never going back!"

Wednesday: "I had a horrible day! Everyone hates me! I'll never have friends!"

Thursday: "Hey, Mom! Want to help me with my lines? I get to be Dorothy in *The Wizard of Oz*! Miss Johnson said I'm a wonderful actress! I can't wait to wear those ruby red slippers."

Friday: "No dinner for me, Mom. I have to lose weight. A boy at school said I was fat. I hate my body."

Quite an emotional roller coaster, isn't it? Next to family, school is the biggest factor in your daughter's life. After all, look at how many hours she spends in the classroom. It's logical that teachers, classmates, lessons, and homework play a big part in your daughter's development. It's our job as parents to try to have school be a positive experience. (Not that there won't by some trying times!)

Here's a sobering fact. According to the American Association of University Women, girls and boys enter school roughly equal in measured ability. In fact, on some benchmarks of school readiness, such as fine motor control, girls are ahead of boys. Yet, 12 years later, girls have fallen behind their classmates in several key areas such as high-level math and measures of self-esteem.

As mothers, we want our daughters to breeze through school with a zest to learn. We want them to have creative teachers willing to see the unique nature of their personalities and learning styles. In reality, your daughter is probably in a class of 28 students with diverse backgrounds and learning abilities. Many educators use the term "educational slide" referring to when girls enter middle school. Instead of enthusiastically waving their arms in the air to answer a question, girls keep their knowledge to themselves. There may be a stigma to being smart. Girls need an extra amount of healthy self-esteem to feel confident to do their best at school.

> *Allie, age 12:* "I liked getting good grades in elementary school. I'd always add some extra sticker or picture to my reports to get extra credit. In middle school, some kids gave me dirty looks when I kept answering the teacher's questions. Now I turn in my homework but don't say much in class."

Your daughter faces challenges in wanting to be a good student but facing negative peer pressure when completing assignments and participating in class. By helping your daughter establish a positive relationship with her teachers, she has a stronger chance of doing well in school.

One mom had a tradition of sending a letter to her daughter's teacher a few days before school started. It wasn't a "My daughter is wonderful, so give her special privileges" letter, but a factual yet heartfelt correspondence. She first of all acknowledged the difficulties teachers face in dealing with so many children with so many needs. Then the letter went on to say something like, "I know you have children with varying skills and capabilities. Here are just a few things I hope you notice in my daughter." Mom went on to describe her daughter's tender spirit, always looking out for a stray animal and befriending children without friends. Teachers appreciated knowing something about her daughter's personality at the beginning of the school year.

Remember the media stir created several years ago when a new talking Barbie said, "Math is sooooo hard"? The educational slide strongly demonstrates itself in the areas of math and science. Tween girls suddenly decide "I can't do math" or "Science class is so boring." In high school, boys outnumber girls two-to-one in advanced physics and chemistry. So, Mom, here's your challenge: find ways to incorporate science and math into your daughter's education.

Many colleges now offer Saturday programs geared for tween girls to experiment with science concepts or take math classes directly related to practical experiences. The Girl Scouts, Boys and Girls Clubs, and park departments all offer technical-style programs designed to keep girls interested in math and science. A study by Girls Inc. showed that when girls were given the chance to perform difficult tasks in science and math, they were just as interested and capable as boys. Can you help the PTA raise money for an after-school math club? How about taking your daughter to a program at the science museum? When your daughter sees that science concepts are a part of her life as much as a dance class, she gains overall self-confidence.

Your daughter's self-confidence may also take a dive when she starts middle school and gets her first low test score. It's a shock for your bright, eager-to-learn daughter to find the work in middle school is suddenly more difficult than grade school. She may immediately feel dumb and unable to keep up with the work. This is the time when her role models (parents and teachers) step in to reassure her about her academic capabilities. Let her know it's okay to ask for help. Offer to sit down with her every day for a few minutes of review. Often, all girls need is a "boost" at the beginning of the year to keep them going strong until summer.

In our survey, we asked girls to "Describe a situation at school that makes you feel uncomfortable." Over and over, girls wrote comments such as "It's awkward when teachers call on me and I don't know the answer," "I feel dumb when I don't understand what the teacher is talking about," or "The teacher covers the material too fast and I'm embarrassed to ask for help."

Tom Loveless, director of the Brown Center on Education Policy, says, "No amount of money or legislation can change the central tenet of learning: the family is the single most important influence." He goes on to add that friends, sports, jobs, and television consume more than 90 percent of the average teen's time outside of school. He suggests reducing each activity by two hours a week, giving more time for homework. As a tween, your daughter probably doesn't have a job, but no doubt she is consumed with sports, enrichment classes, and other activities. Instead of trying to squeeze in a math worksheet between violin lessons and a play date, eliminate a few activities. Your daughter will learn more by giving quality time to homework and reading a book for pleasure than by racing from one activity to another.

Let's get practical and look at ways family influence can help your daughter succeed in school.

- Show your daughter how "learning" is incorporated in everyday activities. Make a grocery list and ask her to use the Sunday paper to find coupons for some of the items. When you go shopping, let her carefully read the coupons to find the corresponding item. Some moms give their daughters half the money saved by using coupons. Now that's practical math!

- Follow through on a goal and earn $5,000! That's right. Tweens can participate in the Tiger Woods Start Something Program and earn money to fulfill a dream.

This on-line program (www.tigerwoodsfoundation.org/startsomething) encourages students between the ages of 8 and 17 to complete a series of activities to earn up to $5,000. This is not a scholarship program, but a way to help students see that by achieving a set of goals, they can fulfill a dream. You can provide the encouragement to get your daughter started on the program. For example, if your budding ballerina wants to attend an expensive dance camp across the country, that's what the Start Something Program is for. Does your daughter want to go to Space Camp or buy a quality musical instrument? Successfully complete the program, and you might get a check in the mail!

• Learn how to use the phone book. What's the difference between the white and yellow pages? Ask your daughter: "Let's say my skin breaks out in pimples. How would I find the phone number of a skin care doctor?" Does she know the term *dermatologist*? What happens when you look up "Doctors"? (Doctors are usually listed under "Physicians.") How do you find out if a local pizza parlor delivers pizzas? Does your tween want a pair of high-priced tennis shoes? Have her look up the number of three athletic shoe stores and ask each for the price of her desired shoes. For some children, this can be a daunting task. Offer encouragement and praise.

• Have her select an article from the newspaper and discuss it at dinner. Sure, students get current-events assignments in school, but this way your daughter learns that current events also influence her family. I frequently find an interesting article from the morning paper and place it on Sondra's placemat where she eats breakfast. This produces comments from her such as, "I can't believe these researchers say teens need nine hours of sleep a night!" or "Why do you think people get addicted to buying lottery tickets like the lady in this article?"

• Watch and discuss a TV show together. Ask your daughter if the characters remind her of her friends. Would she have responded to a situation the same way the TV character did? Ask questions about the commercials. Can Barbie really twirl around as an ice skater the way the commercial shows?

• Show that you are a life-long learner. Let your daughter help you select a community enrichment class you plan to take. Explain how you made the choice to take a gourmet soup-making class rather than one in flower arranging. When reading a book, share a paragraph and ask your daughter what she thinks.

• Express interest in what your daughter learns at school. Granted, studying the export crops of Peru isn't something you look forward to weeks in advance. Ask questions about the map she's coloring. Have her tell you the difference between importing and exporting items. If Grandma comes over, ask your daughter to explain what Lewis and Clark discovered on their expedition.

• Make frequent trips to the library. Sure, your daughter finds facts on the internet, but nothing beats searching library shelves for information. Show your daughter a set of encyclopedias. Many parents tell me their elementary students have never used an encyclopedia. I have fond memories of getting the "D" volume from the *World Book* encyclopedia and spending hours looking at the color pictures of purebred dogs recognized by the American Kennel Club. I'll really date myself by confessing I loved going to my elementary school library and using the card catalog. One mom utilized her library's rotating art collection as a learning tool. The library had a wide selection of Monets, Picassos, Warhols, and other famous paintings (reproductions, of course!). Each week, she'd select a painting to hang on the living room wall and also check out a book about the artist. It was a free way to become familiar with a wide variety of artists.

• Plan casual home activities related to school subjects. I came home one day to find our kitchen turned into a wholesale bakery by my husband Allan and our older daughter Trina. Cookies were cooling on every counter or table space available. Trina, covered in flour, beamed and said, "I never knew fractions could be so easy!" My husband explained that she was having trouble understanding fractions as he helped with homework. "I thought it would be good if she saw how fractions worked, so we decided to make cookies and talk about the fractions in the recipe." Trina's homemade math assignment was to take a recipe that made six dozen cookies and not double it, not triple it, but quadruple the recipe! We then had a math lesson about how many calories were in all the cookies we ate!

• Help your daughter find a topic where she can be an expert. Does she like tap dancing? Encourage her to read a children's biography of famous tap dancers. Take her to a musical like *42nd Street* or *Singin' in the Rain*. Help her compare styles of tap shoes. What does it take to audition on Broadway as a tap dancer? How did tap dancing originate? By learning about a topic in depth, she gains knowledge that most people don't have.

Sondra says: When I was in sixth grade, I decided to participate in this amazing program called National History Day. Thousands of kids across the country participate. The contest gives you a general theme like "Revolution, Reaction, and Reform." Then you can write an essay, make a video, create a huge poster board, or do a dramatic monologue which you write. Oh yes, you have to document at least 50 resources that you used! It's a MAJOR project that took me months.

I used Ethel Merman as an example of a woman who reformed Broadway because she was the first to play strong, powerful women on stage. You have to incorporate facts into the eight-minute monologue you perform. I dressed up in a red dress like Ethel Merman wore when she sang her signature piece, "Everything's Coming Up Roses." She was known for her powerful singing, so I belted out segments of her songs in my monologue. Well, I took first place and was even asked to perform it again during the awards ceremony.

What has really struck me is how all that research about Ethel Merman, Broadway, composers, and the time period has stayed with me. So often, someone will be discussing something and I can add an intelligent comment because I gained so much information from studying one person in depth.

Last week, I was interviewing to get into a competitive drama program this summer. I sat down with the judge, and he said, "Hello, I'm Eric Zimmerman." I immediately asked, "Any relation to Ethel Merman?" He looked at me quizzically and I continued: "Ethel Merman's real name was Ethel Zimmerman. When she was young she knew 'Zimmerman' was too long to fit on a theatre marquee, so she dropped the *Zim* and shortened her name to *Merman*." That broke the ice, and I ended up getting all 10s on my score sheet.

• Encourage family reading as a pleasant pastime, not a punishment. If your daughter is reading a book, find a few ways to embellish the process. When Sondra was in sixth grade, we'd ask her to dress up as a character from the book and give us an oral report. While reading *Gone with the Wind*, she spent a full day sewing an enormous full-skirted dress to wear as she gave her rendition of Scarlett O'Hara. We videotaped it and she actually got extra credit from her English teacher. Have your daughter write a brief letter to a relative, describing the book she's reading. Give her old magazines to make a collage about the book. Show her how CliffsNotes or SparkNotes assist in understanding a book. (You'll probably have to confess how you used CliffsNotes in college when you didn't read a required book.) Help her write a CliffsNotes version of her book. Provide a large piece of poster board so she can draw a map of various locations in the book. Pretend the book has been made into a movie; what kind of movie review would she write?

Hopefully those ideas will show Tom Loveless, the education expert quoted at the beginning of this chapter, that we're all going to incorporate learning into our daily family life! Now comes the time to go the more traditional route and find ways to help your daughter succeed with school-related work.

Mother-Daughter Mini-Activity

Make learning fun by planning a weekly "Family Amazing Fact Night." Each family member needs to use a book, a magazine, the Web, or a newspaper to come up with an interesting fact. Amaze your daughter with such life-changing information as:

Peanuts are one of the ingredients in dynamite.

Almonds are a member of the peach family.

An ostrich's eye is bigger than its brain.

A dime has 118 ridges around the edge.

There are 336 dimples on a regulation golf ball.

Use these facts and your daughter will think you are a genius! (Or she may think you watch too many trivia-based game shows.)

Your daughter spends six to eight hours a day at school. As she enters the front door, you probably start a conversation like this.

Mom: "Haley, do you have any homework?"

Then perhaps you hear a response like this:

Haley: "No. Well, actually, I *did* have homework, but I decided to go to the library and get it done at lunch. Then I wrote my spelling words three times each so I'd be sure to get 100 on my test tomorrow. As soon as I got home from school, I decided not to watch TV and did my social studies worksheet instead. I also drew a map of China for extra credit."

If that conversation sounds familiar ... there's no need to keep reading this book. For most of us, though, the after-school conversation is more like this:

Mom: "Haley, do you have any homework?"
Haley: "No."
Mom: "What about that report on whales you were working on yesterday. Is that done?"
Haley: "Oh, yeah, I forgot. I have to finish that."
Mom: "Didn't you say there was a make-up math worksheet you needed to complete?"
Haley: "Oh, yeah. I forgot. I'll do it after this show."
Mom: "I think you need to get started right now."
Haley: "I will. Right after this show."
Mom: "Haley, please turn off the TV and do homework now."
Haley: "But M-o-o-o-o-m-m-m, this is my favorite show! I promise I'll do homework after this show. And after I call Jenni ..."

You know how the conversation ends. Voices get louder, tears start flowing (sometimes from you), and homework becomes an evil chore.

> *Evelyn, a computer programmer and the mother of an 11-year-old:* "Homework was always a cause of tension in our house. I finally cracked down and set up a strict homework policy. It occurred to me ... I insist my kids wear seatbelts and ride bikes wearing helmets. Why can't I insist they do homework at a certain time and location? I give them a weekly schedule, taking into account tennis practice and Girl Scouts. If the schedule says she needs to be at her desk on Tuesdays from 4:00 PM to 5:00 PM, that's where I expect her to be. If she doesn't have homework, then I quickly give her a fun project like reading about the history of ice cream. The next time we go out, we'll stop for ice cream and she can share the fact that George Washington paid $200 to buy a recipe for ice cream so he could serve it at the White House. Homework is now a part of the after-school routine."

If it worked for Evelyn, maybe it will work for you! Just the idea of homework is controversial. Many parents complain that homework eats up valuable family time. Others say children need more homework to gain academic strength and get into that all-important Ivy League college. The book *The End of Homework* proclaims that homework is destroying families. Further research has shown that homework raises achievement for

6th through 12th graders. In most cases, it looks like homework is here to stay, so let's find ways to make homework less stressful.

> *Natalie, age 12:* "Don't tell my mom this, but she was right. She's making me sit down and do my homework without the TV on. It's different now in class because I know what the teacher is talking about. I like school more." (We promise, Natalie, we won't tell your mom!)

Sondra says: When I was 14, I started a new school. Some girls warned me about the incredible amount of homework the teachers gave. During the first week, I saw a pattern. The teachers would give a homework assignment. Then they'd leave the last 10 minutes of class to either do homework or talk with friends. I wanted to chat, but decided if I really worked hard, I could get almost all the homework assignment done in class. I hardly ever had to take stuff home, yet my friends kept complaining about all the homework.

The National PTA has published a guide called "How to Help Your Child Succeed," which also gives homework tips. Get a copy through www.pta.org. Here are even more ideas:

- Provide a quiet place to study. Yes, that means no TV in the background or the sound of a sibling playing computer games.
- See that your daughter has a desk or table with school supplies. If her desk has a container holding pencils, a ruler, scissors, and markers, she's less likely to wander aimlessly around the house looking for what she needs.
- Offer to show your daughter how to make a brief "To Do" list. In fact, write out her list for her as she dictates it to you. This helps her organize her thoughts, as well as giving you an idea of what she needs to get done.
- If it's a heavy homework night, set a timer so she takes a five-minute break after 15–20 minutes of studying.
- Continue to make positive comments about her progress. "Your map of India is so detailed—you really did a neat job" goes a long way in keeping the forward momentum going.
- Vary the homework policy. If she's been diligent in doing homework for a week, invite a friend over and conduct a mini spelling bee. One mom hired an eighth grader to help her sixth-grade daughter study for her first middle school "final."
- Be available for support—but not to do the assignment. Ask your daughter if she understands the directions. Sometimes clarifying the assignment is all it takes to enable your daughter to do the work.

> *Connie, mother of 9- and 12-year-old daughters:* "I've found my daughters are much more confident in school if they've completed their homework. They know the material and freely share in class. Those times when they neglected homework are the days they come home discouraged about school. I see it as my job to give them the tools to complete homework. Oh, yes! I also make sure their

backpacks are packed and by the front door before they go to bed. That really helps the day start off on a positive note."

Sometimes a few changes in routine are all it takes to help your daughter feel good about school. In our house, I made a "contract" with Sondra that I'd be willing to do minor edits on her papers. The stipulation is that she gives them to me by 7:00 PM the day before she needs them. My philosophy is "No last minute edits!" Now, instead of having her beg me to look over a paper at 6:45 in the morning as she races to school, I casually read the morning paper instead!

Sondra says: Okay, I know time management is not my strongest trait. But I have a busy life! Sometimes I leave things to the last minute. For a while, I'd rush around every morning before school, grabbing my lunch, looking for my backpack, and scrambling to find a pair of shoes. I didn't like the way my day was starting. Much as I hate to admit it, my mom was right. Now I get everything organized the night before. In the morning, my backpack is ready to go and I've even picked out which pair of shoes I'm wearing!

Your tween daughter is going through many changes physically, mentally, and socially. Since school plays such an important part in her life, it makes sense to give her the skills needed to succeed. That way, when she reaches the "educational slide," she'll soon bounce back and once more be at the top.

Just for Fun

Looking to give your daughter a unique educational experience? Try to arrange for her to visit a school different from hers. Perhaps on a teacher's workday at her school, she could spend the day with a friend who attends a private school. Ask a Montessori school if you and your daughter could visit for a few hours. Take her to see a Waldorf school, where children only use natural materials and don't have designated grade levels. Your daughter's world will open up as she sees students learning in different environments from hers.

Chapter 2

What Happened to My Daughter's Sweet Friends?

Wouldn't it be a wonderful world if everyone loved your daughter as much as you do? The bus driver would tell her, "Carrie, it's so nice to have you on the bus. You have a wonderful smile." At school, her teacher would announce, "Look at this wonderful diorama Carrie made. She's so artistic!" as the class nods in agreement and breaks into applause for your daughter. During lunch, girls would maneuver to sit next to her, saying, "Carrie, can you come to my house for a sleepover this weekend? You're so much fun to be with." Even the school nurse would comment, "Carrie, you sure know how to practice good hygiene by sneezing into a tissue!" Everyone loves your daughter!

In reality, she'll have days where the bus driver ignores her, the teacher overlooks her artistic ability, and her peers snub her. Oh, yes, and the school nurse admonishes her for not washing her hands after using the rest room. Not everyone worships your daughter!

All tweens have times when friends bicker and say mean things to each other. At this age, "best friends" change as often as flavors of lip gloss. But what happens when your daughter finds herself being repeatedly picked on by a "mean girl"?

Here's what Amanda from Louisiana learned by her experience dealing with mean girls:

> "Eight years of bullying and an intelligent mother provided me with the skills to take care of my own group of 'mean girls.' I was an overweight, unattractive, middleclass teen in a school of wealthy girls who looked like they belonged to the country club. Needless to say, I didn't fit in. Every morning while forcing myself to get out of bed, I had to prepare

for another day of cruelty, loneliness, and tears. After a bus ride filled with mean jokes and comments, I arrived once again in my own version of hell. Because we were seated in alphabetical order in every class, I was surrounded by the same seven girls in every class except choir. I discovered I loved to sing. It made me feel comfortable with who I was. Finally finding my own beautiful, unique voice helped me escape.

"With the support of my mother—which at the time seemed like nagging—and many prayers for strength, I decided to cantor at church. (For those of you who aren't Catholic, that means I had to stand before a microphone and lead the whole church in every song.) I won't lie—I was terrified. Cantoring meant I'd be putting the real me on display for everyone to see. It'd give them another opportunity to pick on me. True to form, those girls did what they did best, but this time I had the courage to stand up for myself. I told them off, and it felt so amazingly wonderful. Unfortunately, my newfound courage didn't change their meanness, and the misery continued until I graduated from that school. . . .

"I now attend a wonderful high school where I have really great friends who support me and love me just as I am. Several top universities from around the nation are already recruiting me as a sophomore. You may ask where those mean girls are now. They attend a private, all-girls school where they're all just exactly alike and make less-than-perfect grades. I wouldn't trade my eight bad years for anything in the world. As it turns out, Mom was right. It doesn't matter what anyone else thinks or says about me, because in order to be truly happy I have to be true to myself."

Amanda suffered through eight years of torment at school. She may be an extreme situation, yet girls across the country get bullied every day.

We asked girls this question on our surveys: "You might have seen the movie *Mean Girls*. Can you give an example when a 'mean girl' said or did something that really got you upset?" Here are some of their answers:

- "Some girls said that I looked like a freak. I tried not to let it get to me, but it made me feel horrible inside. All I did was go home early and cried myself to sleep."

- "When I was in middle school, girls used to make fun of the way I dressed and call me a baby. They would push me and yell at me in the bathroom."

- "A girl spread a rumor that I had sex with the ugliest guy in school."

- "She said, 'You're very ugly! Your outfit is so disgusting, it makes me want to throw up.'"

- "One mean girl would bully you. She'd sometimes spread rumors and tell everyone your secrets."

- "I was playing soccer with my friends in the park, and some girls driving by screamed, 'Get some clothes on!' I was in a T-shirt and shorts, and it hurt my feelings."

- "One girl pushed my books down and wouldn't help pick them up."
- "Sometimes people call me ugly or b——, but I try to do the best I can with it."
- "Girls started a rumor and said I stuffed my bra."
- "One of my friends told me I was fat and looked bad in makeup and that I couldn't do anything."
- "Some girl had just moved to our school from a rough part of town, and I guess she was kind of insecure, so she took it all out on me like calling me names and looking me up and down like I was an alien."
- "A girl said I was a lesbian."
- "Talking behind my back and trying to make me feel bad."
- "They started a rumor about me that said I paid someone to be my boyfriend."

WHEW!!! Who would want to be a tween with all that negative behavior and bullying taking place with "mean girls"!

Unfortunately, bullying is more common than we'd like to think. According to a 2004 KidsHealth poll, 86 percent of the more than 1,200 9- to 13-year-olds surveyed said they'd seen someone else bullied. Forty-eight percent said they've been bullied themselves, and 42 percent admitted to bullying other kids. A recent article in *Newsweek* had some scary statistics about teenage girls. According to the FBI's Uniform Crime Report, the number of girls ages 10–17 arrested for aggravated assault has doubled over the last 20 years. The number of girls arrested for weapons possession rose 125 percent between 1983 and 2003. Today, one in three juveniles arrested for violent crimes is female.

Bullying takes many forms. Back in the good old days, we assumed a bully was someone who shoved you against your locker and knocked your books to the floor. Today, bullying rears its ugly head in many ways. When boys bully, it's usually physical. They "accidentally" bump their victim in the hall or try to trip them. While the incidence of girls using physical violence is increasing, the majority of female bullying techniques are more subtle. Mean girls exclude their victims from games on the playground or announce, "This table is reserved for popular girls. You can't sit here."

Cyberbullying is quickly becoming a tool for bullies. Girls with any access to instant messaging or e-mail have the ability to spread rumors and tell lies with the click of a key. As schools become more racially diverse, bullies can single out students with ethnic or culture differences. Verbal bullying ranks high as a tool used to make victims feel belittled or degraded. Bullies tend to laugh and mock children they're picking on.

Why do children bully?

Basic psychology tells us that bullies pick on other kids as a way to make themselves feel better. Most bullies have low self-esteem and need to build themselves up by picking on children with even lower self-esteem. Bullies are quick to spot children who have a "weakness." The shy girl in need of braces or a girl that stutters is a perfect target for a bully. Sad as it seems, some young bullies don't even know their behavior is negative. If they have grown up in a home where an adult constantly degrades and bullies children, the bully feels it's normal and acceptable to taunt a weaker child at school. Deborah Prothrow-Stith, author of the book *Sugar and Spice and No Longer Nice* (Jossey-Bass, 2006), says:

The initial causes of violence are found in the early learning experiences in the family, which includes weak family bonding, and ineffective monitoring and supervision. The exposure to and reinforcement for violence in the home, including physical abuse, has a tremendous impact on the potential for later adolescent female violence. (47)

While we can't control what happens in other people's homes, we can help our daughters stand up to a bully. One 12-year-old told me, "I've never had anyone pick on me. Hey! I'm friendly, good at soccer, and know I can talk to my teacher if I have a problem. Oh, yeah. I'm confident in myself. Bullies leave me alone." Now there's a self-assured tween! It's true. Girls with a strong self-image seldom find themselves the victim of bullying.

How do you know if your child is being picked on? Look for some of these signs:

• Your daughter frequently talks about a certain girl at school, pointing out the girl's mean spirit.
• She starts to resist going to a certain class or activity.
• Teachers comment that your daughter is having difficulty concentrating in class.
• She seems more withdrawn than usual.
• She races home to go the bathroom, since she won't go at school.
• She begs you to take her to school, avoiding the bus.
• She's hungry because she "lost" her lunch money.
• You notice she's having nightmares.

If you suspect your daughter is being bullied, help her share her fears and frustrations. Avoid telling her, "Just stand up to that girl. Don't be such a baby!" Spend time with your daughter, letting her vent. It's so tempting to step in with well-meaning, motherly advice when really your daughter simply needs to talk. If she seems reluctant to discuss the situation (and you know she's not in danger), wait a few days. Then bring up a general question such as, "I read a newspaper article that talked about girls getting bullied at school. Do any of your friends ever get bullied?" Ask what her friends do when threatened by a bully.

In our surveys, girls shared their techniques for coping with a bully. These included:

- "Stand up for yourself. Don't let her talk about you and make you feel bad. Let her know the stuff she says to you isn't going to get you down."
- "The best thing to do is confront her about it so you can get it out there in the open."
- "Just let it roll off your back and pretend it doesn't affect you."
- "Think of something clever to say that minimizes the mean girl."
- "Always be extra nice. Go out of your way to be extremely nice. For instance, always saying hi."
- "Realize and believe you do not always have to lower yourself to their level. Sometimes taking action is the last thing you should do, but internally recognizing your worth is the best way to fight a mean girl."
- "Normally I just ignore her, but I will admit I've beaten the crap out of a few mean girls."
- "Ignore them. It's not about what other people think of you. It's what you think about yourself."
- "Usually I don't think it always matters what you say. It is the fact that you know you have the power to forgive and that makes you a good person. The best reaction is to hold your head high."
- "Just find a really good friend to help you through or talk to a grown-up."

Most of these girls have not only experienced bullying but have also tried various solutions. Since bullies prey on weaker students, it's important that your daughter develop self-confidence. Other chapters in this book give ideas on raising your daughter's self-esteem and giving her a "go get 'em" attitude.

If your daughter confides that she's being bullied, help her with some of these coping skills:

- Bullies feel powerless, so they want to exert power over another child. If your daughter cries, or shirks away, the bully has gained power. As many of the girls in the surveys stated, simply walking away confidently is a good solution. The bully isn't getting any satisfaction because her victim isn't showing weakness. Role-play various situations so she feels comfortable looking the bully in the eyes and then striding away. Even better is if your daughter learns to make eye contact with the bully and say, "I won't listen to you talking to me like that!" before walking away.
- Encourage your daughter to have a friend with her at those times when the bully is likely to provoke. There's comfort in walking into the cafeteria with a friend, knowing a bully is less likely to attack two girls together.
- Does your daughter see the bully only at a specific club or activity? Sometimes it's easiest to simply remove your daughter from that environment. As one

mother said: "My 10-year-old daughter is confident and gets along well with all her classmates at school. Gymnastics is another situation. For six months, one girl constantly picked on Amanda, even after Amanda confronted her and the teacher monitored the situation. I talked to the bully and her mother, but the girl kept saying mean and cutting remarks to Amanda. We finally decided to move to another afternoon for gymnastics class, and that solved the problem."

- Encourage your daughter to tell a teacher, counselor, or principal. Sometimes a meeting with a few adults and the bully will bring the situation under control. Many schools now have antibullying policies in place.

Mother-Daughter Mini-Activity

Get a large piece of newspaper and trace around your daughter's body. Help her draw in facial features and a few clothes so it looks like she's wearing a T-shirt and pants. Now it's time to decorate the paper T-shirt she's wearing. Have her list all her positive traits while you write them on the shirt. List characteristics such as "smart," "musical," "kind," "good sense of humor," "friendly," and so on. Hang the self-portrait where she can look at it and see words reinforcing her strong characteristics.

In all cases, if your daughter shows signs of distress and fear, it's time to step in and take action. Your daughter gains coping skills by learning to deal with a bully, but she should never have to handle a situation dealing with a dangerous, emotionally disturbed child.

My good friend Susan Fee conducts training for both parents and girls on various aspects of mean girls. She's also a licensed counselor and the author of *My Roommate Is Driving Me Crazy! Solve Conflicts, Set Boundaries, and Survive the College Roommate from Hell*. She may be contacted through her website, www.susanfee.com.

Here's an article Susan wrote for the *Cleveland/Akron Family* that gives more practical information on helping your daughter deal with a bully.

Mean Girls Behavior Damaging

In a few weeks my daughter will begin first grade. I want to believe that she can handle a full day away from my protective care, but I'm worried. Right now, she's confident, bubbly, and expressive. I'm not ready for her to have her heart and spirit broken—by another girl. Yet, according to researchers and experts on girl aggression, that's mostly likely what will happen.

A recent study conducted by Brigham Young University suggests girls as young as 3 or 4 will use manipulation and peer pressure to get what they want. They regularly exclude others and threaten to withdraw friendship if they don't get their way. They are mean girls in training.

The popularity of the movie *Mean Girls* gave a public voice to something that women have known for years: girls can be cruel. But the way girls dish it out is very different from the physical aggression displayed by boys.... While dirty looks may seem less harmful than physical aggression, ... the psychological consequences can be dramatic. ...

Why is it girls treat one another this way? Even more confounding, why do they want to be friends with girls who would treat them poorly? In her book *Queen Bees and Wannabes*, author Rosalind Wiseman describes a complex social system that teaches girls it's better to be "nice" than outwardly express anger, so girls learn to assert their power in more subtle ways. Mothers, who grew up with same social pressures, can unwittingly reinforce the message.

For example, if a daughter witnesses her mom giving the "cold shoulder" she learns the way you express anger is by cutting off communication. If the mother openly gossips, she teaches that passive-aggressive behavior is acceptable. Or, imagine a scenario where a mom receives poor customer service, but chooses not to address it because she doesn't want to "make a scene."

The other message girls receive according to Wiseman is that it's better to be included than left out, even if inclusion hurts. Girls exclude by withholding friendships, such as not inviting someone to a birthday party or forming cliques.

Wallace said she sees this behavior played out in an unending cycle. "Most girls return to the group or friend that hurt them. They'd rather be picked on that kicked out and suffer the pain of social isolation."

I interviewed several girls for this article. While all of them wanted to talk about their experiences, none of them wanted to be identified for fear that they would be picked on even more. Their stories had much in common including engaging in the very behavior they found so hurtful. One 14-year-old told me, "Sometimes I respond by being catty right back. At first, I feel slightly triumphant and then I feel guilty." The same girl experienced a painful falling out with her best friend after an online exchange, which is the newest trend in relational aggression.

Hi-tech bullying includes flaming, which is sending angry, rude, or vulgar messages directed at a person, privately or to an online group. Some online users masquerade as someone else, or spread gossip through online personal diaries called blogs. Most often, it's the intentional exclusion from an Instant Messaging "buddies list" that causes hurt feelings. Parry Aftab is a cyber lawyer and executive director of WiredSafety.org. She strongly encourages parents to Google their child's name, nicknames, friends' names, and school name to alert them to unreported cyberbullying.

There are other things parents can do to help their daughters survive relational aggression. First, avoid minimizing the situation. Offering over-simplified advice such as, "Get new friends," and "None of this will matter when you're older," will only make girls feel more misunderstood.

Do not intervene on your daughter's behalf or tell her to ignore it. This saves her from learning valuable conflict resolution skills and can inadvertently make her feel even more powerless. Instead, Wallace suggests girls learn how to confront their perpetrators individually by using the sentence, "When you _____ I feel _____ and I'd appreciate it if _____."

If your daughter isn't much of a talker you might bring up the topic by asking, "How do the girls at school treat one another?" It's also very powerful for mothers to share their own girlhood experiences. I know I have a few painful stories to tell. As much as I'd like to forget them, being honest about my past may be the very thing my daughter needs for her future.

While you worry your daughter might be the victim of a bully, other moms are worrying that *their* daughter *is* the bully. Lauren, the mother of a 12-year-old living in Ohio, said: "My daughter's always been assertive and bossy. I have to work hard to teach her not to push her way around. She's not really mean, just wants her own way. I worry she'll turn into a real mean girl when she hits the teen years."

As moms, we sometimes worry about our daughters suddenly and viciously turning into female Rambos and picking on innocent girls. Take heart, says James Garbarino in his book *See Jane Hit: Why Girls Are Growing More Violent and What Can Be Done about It*. He tells us that 80 percent of children avoid "dramatic tumultuous change" as they enter adolescence. Other research shows that characteristics developed in childhood carry over to the teen years. Second-graders who swear and push classmates off the slide still use foul language and bully in middle school. Many high school dropouts are the same students who struggled with fourth-grade math. The traits a child develops in early childhood carry on through middle and high school. So, if your daughter was basically a happy well-adjusted child, the odds are she'll continue to be a semi-happy, semi-well-adjusted tween!

Up until the age of 3, boys and girls are equally aggressive. I remember Sondra knocking kids down to get to her favorite playground toy. Since girls develop verbal capabilities faster than boys, however, your preschool daughter soon found other, nonaggressive ways to get what she wanted. Her physical aggression diminished as her ability to use language increased. And, although things are changing, there's still the age-old notion that little girls shouldn't hit because it's not "ladylike."

If you suspect your daughter is beginning to bully other children, it's time to take action. Begin by letting her know bullying is unacceptable behavior. Explain exactly what it means to be a "mean girl." If she doesn't invite Sydney to her birthday party, does that mean she's a bully? Set up standards for acceptable and unacceptable behavior. Find outlets for your daughter to achieve positive recognition. Is she athletic? How about trying a karate or kickboxing class? These programs stress physical activities along with inner self-control.

Talk with teachers and school officials. You may think your daughter is a bully when they see her as a leader. On the other hand, you may praise your daughter's take-charge approach, while her teacher is worried your daughter displays signs of bullying. Margie, a court reporter and mother of a 12-year-old, said: "I was shocked when the teacher asked to talk to us about Annie's bullying behavior. My daughter isn't mean! Yet the teacher had a list of instances where Annie was deliberately singling out certain girls and telling them they couldn't sit at certain tables at lunch and even which computers they could and couldn't use." If there's that gut feeling in your stomach your daughter has mean girl tendencies, check with a teacher. They have a handle on the day-to-day behavior of your daughter among her peers.

Yes, it would be nice if we could go back to the days when your daughter was a toddler, grabbing another child's toy in the sandbox. We would gently return the toy, saying, "Emma, use your words to tell Sara you want the shovel. Let's share these toys." In the meantime, give your daughter the skills she needs to be self-confident in herself as a person. Hopefully that way she won't need to be a bully or let herself be one.

Instead of having Sondra give a few scattered thoughts throughout this chapter, we decided to have her write this section of the chapter directly to your daughter. Next time the two of you have some spare time, casually sit down and read these few pages together. Don't forget to serve the root beer floats!

Sondra says: What do you think when you hear the phrase "school bully"? The image that comes to mind is probably a sweaty football player with bad breath and pimples, strutting in his letterman's jacket. He's flanked by two sidekicks who randomly stuff underclassmen into the garbage cans.

Although this type of bully is often seen on television shows, there's another image that's harder to spot. This bully usually wears the latest fashions and has perfectly highlighted hair. She seems to have "her act together" and plenty of friends. These miniskirted bullies can make a girl's life just as miserable as the other kind. They're known as "mean girls." They might look sweet and innocent, but they have a way of saying things that make you feel bad for days.

In early elementary school, we'd chant, "Sticks and stones can break your bones, but words can never hurt you." Then, along about fourth grade, we changed it to "Sticks and stones can break your bones, and words can break your heart." I guess we were learning that words really can damage a person's spirit. You may sit in class feeling happy and upbeat because of a good grade on your history test. Then Miss Mean waves your test in the air and announces, "Isn't this sweet? Ashley's so smart. She knows all about the Civil War. That's because she studies alone on Saturday nights instead of going to parties." You feel embarrassed and mad. Her words stay with you for a long time. You may even consider letting your grades drop so she won't tease you again. (Not a good idea!)

Can you think of a time when someone made fun of you because you did something well? Did you get the lead in a school play maybe, or get a good grade on a test? What did the person say? How did you handle the situation? How do you *wish* you had handled the situation?

> *Jan, age 13:* "I have dealt with quite a few unpleasant females for much of my life. It all starts at a very early age. First, girls do petty things such as cutting in line, and not sharing toys. Next, they begin to psychically abuse and say hurtful things. I have been called 'skinny'

on numerous occasions, made fun of because of clothing, hair, and anything else they could find. However, those are the things that we forget."

"M," *age 16:* "Many times girls are behaving in a 'mean' way but are not even aware of it. Clans are formed. Rumors are spread. You become outcast from it all. You are supposedly 'friends' with a group, but they don't treat you as a friend. You don't do things with them that they all do together as a group. They think you don't see it. They think you're not hurt. They think you don't care, when all you can do is wish that you could be accepted. That is what hurts the most—not being included. That's when people attempt to change, thinking it will pull it all together, when everything just falls apart. No one can deceive for long and attempt to conceal all the pain that's buried deep down inside. Females need to come together and stop tearing each other apart. We are all very unique and different. We all have different life stories. But if you look close enough, even a blind person can see that we all have similar qualities. All need attention and affection. We all want to be accepted by someone, even if we don't stand right up and say it. When people try to change themselves, nothing much is accomplished. Just precious time is wasted and precious energy."

As my mom and I surveyed hundreds of girls, it's amazing for me to see how girls across the country get picked on by others. Here's what a Lisa from California wrote:

"When I was in eighth grade, there was a mean girl named Yolanda, who for some reason had it out for me. All her friends would follow me and call me names. Then they progressed to trying to trip me or block my way in the halls between classes. Finally, they threw gum in my hair. I was scared and didn't know what to do. So I talked to my mom, and she told me to try talking, and if that did not work, to be ready to back it up.

Well, the next day Yolanda and her gang surrounded me by my gym locker. I was sweating and shaking, but I managed to find my voice. I told her that I really did not want to fight. Well, Yolanda was quiet. And so were her girls. And then she just laughed and we shook hands.

From then on, Yolanda and her girls had my back. When I ran for office, they campaigned for me. It was the weirdest thing. I am not sure why they changed their minds, but it did show me that if you are faced with a scary situation, sometimes the solution is to face it head on."

In many cases, like Lisa's, you don't know why someone is being mean to you. Wouldn't it be easer if someone who you didn't like just came up to you and said, "Anna, I don't like you because you have cuter clothes than I do"? If we knew why someone was being mean, we could either fix it or at least understand why she is so mean.

Often girls just act weird. Other times they have an issue with something that you have done to them. Maybe there's a problem at home or a situation at school they are dealing with. That's what's so confusing about dealing with school bullies. They might be mean to you one day and then two days later act like you are best friends.

Let's take a quick test to see what real friendship means. True or false:

- A good friend sticks up for you when others cut you down.
- A good friend lets you rant and rave over something you think is important but doesn't really matter to her.
- A good friend keeps the secrets you've told her.
- A good friend apologizes if she's hurt your feelings.
- A good friend accepts you for who you are. She doesn't tell you to lose weight or listen to a certain type of music.

Hopefully you answered "true" for each statement. Everyone is in a bad mood now and then, but real friends don't deliberately try to make you feel bad or insecure about yourself. So, if a girl spends four days making you feel miserable and then acts like she's your friend, watch out!

Let's talk about that girl that is making your life miserable. What do you do when she starts picking on you? I think there are three main ways to handle the situation.

Strategy #1: Ignore the person. Sometimes this is hard to do, especially if she sits next to you in English and you have assigned seats. In a best-case scenario, a girl who is mean to you wants to see you get upset. Sometimes ignoring her wrecks her plan. Since she can't get a reaction out of you, she might just leave you alone and start picking on another person. So, as soon as the mean girl starts her attack, walk away or act as if what she said doesn't bother you. I know it *will* bother you, but keeping a calm attitude might be enough for her to leave you alone.

Here are what some girls your age have done when it comes to getting bullied:

- "I would walk off and try and ignore the girl, and if she wouldn't stop, just tell her to quit."
- "Ignore them, because if you stop acting like you care, they won't bother you. I've learned that through experience. It really does work."
- "Just walk away and be the bigger person."

For the past several years, I've been a spokesperson for a Christian relief agency called Childcare Worldwide. Because of this, I've visited their programs in Peru, Africa, and Mexico. I don't really say too much about it, but the word somehow gets out that I travel a lot and have written six books. At my new school, one girl decided she didn't like that I did volunteer work for kids in developing countries. She started out by saying, "So, are you off to save another rain forest today?" and "Going to be on TV again and brag how wonderful you are saving the world?" Then her comments got meaner and meaner. Other girls would watch to see my reaction. I decided to simply ignore her. Naturally I wanted to yell, "Don't you understand I'm raising money so kids in Africa can go to school and get an education?" Instead, I kept a "neutral" face and walked away. Within a few weeks, she stopped her negative remarks. In my case, ignoring her worked.

However, in one of our surveys, a girl wrote how she tried ignoring a mean girl and it didn't work.

> *Christa, age 13:* "It was around Christmas and all was going well for me in middle school. I liked singing in the school choir and was getting pretty good grades. My friends and I hung out together with few problems. One day in math class, a girl I had sat next to for three months looked at me and said, 'You're gaining weight. Won't be long until you are real fat.' I ignored her. The next day she 'accidentally' knocked my book to the floor. All of a sudden, for no reason she made my life miserable. She constantly bugged me in class and made me feel miserable. I thought ignoring it would make her stop, but it didn't. I went through the rest of the year with her bothering me. Now I hate math and I hate her."

Strategy #2: Have a plan. If ignoring doesn't work, try something else. You are smart, so use your intelligence to outwit the mean girl. If you know she's going to slam your locker shut as she walks to PE, go to your locker earlier. She'll soon cross "Slam Jessica's locker" off her list if she sees you aren't there. It's not that you are scared of her—you are just stopping her pattern of mean behavior.

Have a plan to react unemotionally to her comments. There are times when the mean girl will say something really hurtful. You might even want to cry. Plan ahead to sing a song in your head or think about something positive so her mean words won't upset you. If the mean girl sees your eyes starting to tear up, she thinks, "Ah! Success! I got Jessica to cry." Don't give her that power.

Have a plan also about what to say. Have your mom help you rehearse sentences and phrases to say. Practice as if you were in a play. If a mean girl constantly criticizes your clothes, know exactly what you'll say when she says, "Looks like your mom bought that blouse at the thrift shop."

Your plan might also involve being nice to the person tormenting you. It's hard! Here's what 16-year-old Alison wrote on her survey:

> "Two years ago when I was in eighth grade, I was assigned to do a project with a girl in my class. She was the only person I knew in that class and we were somewhat of friends. Our project was to make a bridge out of balsa wood. At first she was nice, but as the days went by she started treating me like I was stupid and had no idea what I was doing. She called me names like "idiot" and "moron." The way I dealt with this girl was just being nice to her; I didn't try to do the same things to her. Whenever she called me names, I would think I'm not like that, this is just her opinion. Something must have changed, because now we are in ninth grade and are able to talk and work on projects together without her making me feel stupid and bad about myself."

Strategy #3: Ask for help if the situation is getting dangerous. It's very important that you have friends you can rely on and who can help you through the things going on in your life. Everyone should have someone their own age that they can trust. However, it's also important to have someone who is older than you to help if the bullying seems to be getting out of hand. Although at times you feel like you are mature enough to handle anything, an older person who has experience can give a different perspective. Sometimes you can go to your parents, even though you think parents have trouble relating to what's actually going on in today's schools (although you'd be surprised how much they do know). A teacher or youth group leader can also be a great person to help you.

Here's a situation that ended after an "authority figure" stepped in.

> *Alex, a 10-year-old from Missouri:* "Once at lunch my best friend Micki and I would sit at our lunch table in our own little area. These other girls thought they were better than us because of their color decided to try and make our whole lunch period miserable. First they would throw apples at us and yell mean words at us. Then they told us that if we didn't stop sitting at their table they would beat us up. Micki and I got very nervous and did not know what to do. Finally we told the teacher and she separated them. They never have been mean to us again! I think it was because they were in a group that they tried to show off and be mean."

Here are some ways to tell if the situation is getting dangerous:

- The mean girl threatens to "hurt you real bad."
- She shoves you or tries to physically hurt you.
- She sends threatening messages to you on your e-mail or IM.
- Her friends start telling you to watch out because the mean girl really hates you.

Tell an adult anytime the situation gives you that gut-level feeling that the mean girl is serious. Don't worry that telling will make her even more mad. You need to protect yourself from girls who have real problems.

Mother-Daughter Mini-Activity

Here's a mini-activity to do: Pretend you are filling out the survey that my mom and I sent to girls around the country. How would you answer this question?

Please describe a time when you felt a mean girl or a bully was picking on you. What did you do? Do you think you handled the situation in the best way?

Have your mom answer this question:

Think back to when you were a tween. Please describe a time when you felt a mean girl or a bully was picking on you. What did you do? Do you think you handled the situation in the best way?

When you are done, share your situations with each other.

Just for Fun

That's enough on this serious issue! Let's end with a little fun. Try this craft project with your daughter. It's the perfect activity for "mindless" crafting where you can be decorating the candle while having a conversation with your daughter about bullying.

Here's what you'll need:

- Assorted candles, available at any dollar store (fat, stubby candles work better than tapers)
- Needles with round colored "heads". These can be found at craft stores in the quilting department or go to an office supply store and look for "map" pins.
- Sequins in various colors. Feel free to experiment. Most sequins are round, but star shaped or oval sequins are also available.
- Metal spoon

Follow these easy steps:

1. You really don't need too many complicated directions for this project. Simply stick a pin through the hole in the sequin.
2. Good! Now stick the pin into the candle.
3. Repeat steps 1 and 2 over and over and over until you have the design you want (or until you get bored pushing pins into a candle). Some people find that their fingers get sore pushing the pins in the wax. That's where your spoon comes in handy. Use the back of the spoon to put pressure on the pin head and get it all the way into the candle.

That's all there is to it. You'll end up with a designer sparkly candle plus the opportunity to have a non-eye-contact conversation with your daughter!

Chapter 3

I'm So Tired of Repeating Myself, Repeating Myself, Repeating Myself

Camille, computer analyst and frustrated mom: "Why is it I have to tell my 12-year-old daughter Melissa something 25 times before she listens? It gets so frustrating to ask her to take out the trash again and again. All I do is harp on her. If she'd just do what I ask (and I don't ask that much from her). Yesterday I was busy because my younger son was sick. I asked Melissa to feed the dog. Naturally she says, 'I will in a minute.' Half an hour later, my son is vomiting and the dog is looking at me, waiting to be fed. I asked Melissa three more times to feed the dog before I got really upset and started yelling. She grudgingly got up and threw some dry food in the poor dog's bowl. Can't she do it the first time I ask? It only takes 30 seconds to feed the dog."

Mothers often feel like the proverbial broken record, repeating themselves over and over. (Wait! Does your daughter even know what a record looks like? There's a great mother-daughter activity—go to an antique store and show your daughter how you used to listen to the Beach Boys on a vinyl album.)

Our daughters stop listening to us because all too often we never stop talking. Melissa probably tuned out her mom's pleading to feed the dog. She also assumed that if she ignored her mom long enough, good old mom would eventually feed the dog herself.

Think about a typical morning at your house. Does it go something like this?

"Time to get up, Allie.... Allie, you're going to be late. I'm not taking you to school if you miss the bus.... Hurry up; your sister wants to use the bathroom.... Where's your backpack? I told you to put it by the door.... Why didn't you pack it last night?... Allie, don't eat cookies for breakfast...."And so on. Even if you had said, "I'm doubling your allowance," Allie wouldn't have noticed, since she stopped listening long ago. Here's what one 11-year-old wrote in our survey:

> "I have it figured out. If I ignore my mom when she tells me to do something, she'll say it again and again and again. Then she does it herself or gets my sister to do it. So if she asks me to take out the trash, I don't say anything. Then I don't have to do the trash."

Now that's a perceptive preteen!

Sondra says: I hate to admit it, but I do tune out my mom. When she is repeating something over and over and over again, I won't listen to her anymore. What is really helpful for me is when she makes clear lists. She can tell me 10 times to make a phone call, but I'm just going to assure her with, "Don't worry about it, I'll get it done," and then I forget who I was suppose to call a minute later. Making out a clear, succinct list helps me monitor my own time and get everything done. It gives the responsibility to me and makes me feel accomplished when I finish, rather then just feeling like I'm always behind because my mom keeps reminding me.

Several years ago, Allan and I visited a family with three children. It seemed like a typical home with a few toys on the floor, comfortable furniture, and a refrigerator covered with lunch menus and photographs. After a few minutes of chatting, the mother called her children to dinner. Twelve-year-old Stephanie answered, "I'll be there in a minute. I'm just finishing making this bracelet." Obviously this reply did not suit Stephanie's mother. She strode into her room and yelled, "Stephanie! When I call you, I expect you to come. I demand instant obedience!"

Mom returned to the kitchen. A few minutes passed, and still no sign of Stephanie. Clearly Stephanie wasn't concerned about being instantly obedient. Once more Mom yelled, "That's it, Stephanie. Get down here right now or you are in big trouble." Stephanie must have been very engrossed in her jewelry-making because her mother yelled several more times to come to dinner. We got the feeling Stephanie had no fear about getting in "big trouble."

Finally, in exasperation, Mom decided to start the meal without her. Halfway through dinner, Stephanie sauntered to the table, demanding her food. Mom launched into a long lecture about the importance of coming when called, being respectful, acknowledging her work at preparing a meal—you get the picture. But while giving the lecture, she returned to the kitchen to heat up Stephanie's dinner! Stephanie received extra attention by refusing to come to dinner on time.

Any other ways to handle the situation? Let's look at a few scenarios.

Scenario #1. You announce to your daughter that dinner will be on the table in five minutes. She stops making jewelry and says, "Mom, let me help you. Can I set the table or pour milk? I can finish making these bracelets later. You know I'm going to sell them and give the money to charity, don't you? The important thing now is that I help you with dinner. I'll clean up afterwards also." Okay, *that* will never happen as long as preteens are on the planet. It's a nice fantasy, though, isn't it?

Scenario #2. Ten minutes before dinner, Mom goes to Stephanie's room and looks at the bracelets she's making. Mom says, "I'll call you in five minutes to wash your hands and come to dinner. Why don't you bring your bracelet and show it to the rest of the family while we eat?" Five minutes before dinner, Mom goes to Stephanie's room and gently touches her on the shoulder, reminding her it's time to come to dinner. Stephanie washes her hands, brings her sparkly bracelet to the table, and the meal starts in a relaxed setting. (Don't laugh! I've seen mothers with large families use this technique, and it works! It just takes extra effort on your part to physically touch and remind your daughter to come to dinner.)

Scenario #3. Ten minutes before dinner, Mom goes to Stephanie's room and looks at the bracelets she's making. Mom says, "I'll call you in five minutes to wash your hands and come to dinner. Why don't you bring your bracelet and show it to the rest of the family while we eat?" Five minutes before dinner, Mom goes to Stephanie's room and gently touches her on the shoulder, reminding her it's time to come to dinner. Just before dinner, Mom gives one last call of, "Stephanie, we're starting dinner in one minute." A minute later, the family sits down at the table, without Stephanie. A pleasant conversation takes place until 10 minutes later when Stephanie storms in, complaining that she's starving. Mom calmly says, "We've already started dinner. There's extra food on the kitchen counter and you can eat there." Stephanie argues that the food is cold. Mom calmly repeats the message that she can eat the extra food on the counter and that they expect her to eat alone in the kitchen. There's no yelling or arguing. Stephanie is getting her dinner. She simply needs to serve herself and eat alone.

Stephanie will likely groan about the cold food, her mean mother, and so forth. She is, however, learning that if she wants to eat hot food with the family, she needs to be on time. It may take two or three missed mealtimes for Stephanie to get the message to come to dinner when she's called. Then guess what? Suddenly mealtime is a semi-calm hour where the family gathers together for conversation and food. Studies show that students living in families who eat dinner together at least four times a week have higher grades and a closer relationship with their parents. Maybe it's worth a few cold meals to get the family to eat together.

Your daughter probably doesn't listen because there's no need to. She knows you'll repeat the message until she's ready to hear it. We've actually trained our daughters not to listen to us! (And trained them well!) Here's how Lillian, a retail clerk in Cleveland, found a way to stop repeating herself.

> "I could yell until I'm hoarse and my 12-year-old daughter just shuts me out. The louder I yell, the more she ignores me. She doesn't even have the nerve to yell back. If I remember from Psychology 101, she's being passive-aggressive. Maybe I should have paid more attention in that college class so I'd have a better idea how to handle my daughter. Anyway, I found the best way to get my point across on important issues is to write her notes. I'll put a note in her lunch bag that says, 'Please be sure all your chores are done by 4:30 this afternoon.' Then I leave the same note on the front door where she comes in the house. Even though I'm at work, I know she's read the notes and has no excuse to not get her chores done. I don't write notes for everything, just a few major issues."

Lillian has a great idea! So if you are tired of yelling, try leaving clear, concise notes in places your daughter is sure to read them. One mother used humor to convey the message of her notes. She'd attach a note to the vacuum cleaner (on bright pink paper, of course) and place the vacuum in front of the refrigerator. The note said something like:

Gabby, I'm tired of feeling like no one cares about me. I'd be so happy to suck up some dirt if you would just turn me on and vacuum the living room. Could you make a vacuum cleaner ecstatically happy by using me to vacuum the living room by 5:00 PM today? Thanks so much. It would really help my self-esteem to be used for such a worthwhile activity.
Your friend, Vinny the Vacuum

Remember, you're the mother. It's up to you to be creative in communicating to your daughter. If writing notes impersonating a vacuum cleaner saves you from yelling, then give yourself a pen name and start writing!

Sondra says: Oh, yes. I know about notes! I find notes in all sorts of places around the house. My mom's favorite is to tape a note covering the entire TV screen that says, "Sondra, feel free to watch TV as soon as your clothes are all hung up and your bathroom sink, toilet, and shower are clean." I actually like the notes. They are clear and let me know what to do without my mom repeating herself and asking if I heard her. I go to some friends' house, and it gets a bit annoying to hear moms say something over and over. They'll ask if my friend has done her homework ... then ask for details on every subject ... then ask about upcoming assignments, etc. Even I start tuning out—and it's not even my mom talking.

Written communication also works well when it comes to setting rules. Lynn, a training director in Nashville, found a way to keep from having to repeat family rules over and over and over and . . .

> "I remember when the 'negotiations' started. We found that creating a written contract worked well, so that my husband and I and my daughter were all clear about what we agreed were the rules of our household, and consequences for failing to live up to those rules. This prevented us from being inconsistent in our yeses and noes and from being manipulated by a relentless 12-year-old."

Mother-Daughter Mini-Activity

Get some cute stationery at the dollar store. Tell your daughter you'd like to have a Week of Written Communication with her. Show her how you'll replace nagging with short notes. If she forgets to take out the trash, you'll place a reminder note by her plate at dinner. Don't forget to leave some "I love you!" notes for her. Have your daughter communicate with notes also. She could leave you a note asking to go to Tiffany's sleepover on Friday night. Maybe she'll write telling you she thinks you're a great mom! (Save it for your scrapbook!) At the end of the week, discuss the pros and cons of communicating with notes. She may tell you she prefers getting reminder notes to clean her room rather than hearing you tell her again and again and again.

For those times when writing a note isn't appropriate, try another technique to get your daughter to listen. Talk less. Yes, hard as it sounds, the less you say, the more likely your daughter will listen instead of shutting you out. Younger children need longer explanations about getting ready on time or the importance of wearing a seatbelt. But with any luck, your tween daughter by now has the skills to know basic routines and rules.

If backseat squabbling is a problem, try this solution. The next time everyone is in the car, make eye contact and calmly say, "From now on, when you argue and distract me from driving, I'm going to say, 'First warning.' After that, if I hear more squabbling, I will simply pull over to the side of the road and wait until I'm assured you kids can get along. See, I even stocked the car with magazines to read while I'm waiting. If you are late to school, I will not write a note. It's up to you to deal with tardiness. Alyssa, please repeat what I said so I know you understand."

Alyssa, who is wondering what happened to her nagging mom, repeats the instructions. From there, it's easy. The next time your daughter and a sibling are playing the "Mom, Jordan's looking at me cross-eyed" game, declare, "First warning." There's nothing wrong with distracting the nitpicking by starting a lively conversation or even asking for some new knock-knock jokes. However—and here's the big however—if arguing continues, pull over at the first safe place and start reading your magazine. Inconvenient? Most likely. Will your daughter be late for school or dance class? Most likely. Will she get the message you won't tolerate fighting in the car? Most likely. The point is you are saying less while getting the results you want. No more repeating yourself over and over.

Along with saying less, try speaking in shorter sentences. Telling your daughter, "Jenni, you need to be ready for school in 10 minutes. You know you are always late for school, and I'm tired of writing you notes. Did you pack your backpack yet? Why don't you have shoes on? . . . ," is using too many words. Try saying, "Jenni, I'll be in the car at 8:10 to take you to school. Please be on time." At 8:09, walk to the car and simply wait. If Jenni shows up on time, congratulate her and have a pleasant conversation on the way to school. If Jenni is late, have a pleasant conversation on the way to school anyway (although it will be one-sided as she cries about being late) and let her deal with tardiness on her own. In some cases, it helps to call the school ahead of time and let them know the time-management program you're implementing. It doesn't take long for your daughter to begin to listen if you speak in direct, short sentences.

Speaking of pleasant conversations in the car, how about astounding your daughter with some amazing bits of trivia such as:

- Pigs and light-colored horses can get sunburned.
- A housefly beats its wings about 20,000 times per minute.
- Tom Cruise's birth name is Thomas Cruise Mapother IV.
- In Wales, there are more sheep than people.

Here's what one preteen—a 12-year-old who doesn't want to give her name because she's embarrassed to be reading about dead people—said about her mom's attempt to have conversation in the car.

> "My mom is weird. Totally weird and strange. She read some sort of parenting article about how parents should let their kids know about the lives of interesting people. I think that meant we should read a book on George Washington. Not my mom. Every day when we go to school, she hands me the 'Obituary of the Day.' She cuts out an obituary from the morning newspaper. Then I'm supposed to read it to her, and we talk about what the person's life was like. It's kind of creepy, but now I see some people do interesting things."

So what's better for fostering a mother-daughter relationship? Repeating yourself 32 times to get everyone in the car on time, or discussing the life of a deceased man in your community who studied endangered animals on the Galapagos Islands?

As mothers, we feel—no, we *know*—that words of wisdom and knowledge simply flow from our mouths. When dealing with tweens, though, sometimes it's better to keep some of that extensive knowledge to ourselves. The next time you find yourself going into repeat mode, try stepping back. Say what you mean in shorter sentences. Then say those shorter sentences less often. Your daughter will soon learn it's to her advantage to listen when you say something important. (And isn't everything we say important?)

Positive communication results in a closer relationship with your daughter.

> *Cynthia, a therapist and mother to a 12-year-old:* "She is still open to sharing with me about her friends, concerns, and values my opinions (most of the time). She still seeks my guidance on life issues such as puberty, values, sex, etc. She is still more influenced by us than her peers, and has a heart's desire to do what is right."

Isn't that what we all want when it comes to communication?

Okay, you follow through on your statements, speak in shorter sentences, and write notes. Still looking for a few more ideas on communicating with your daughter? How about (get ready—this is hard) *not talking at all.* In other words, try listening as your daughter shares the agony she experienced because she accidentally sat next to Gabby, who was mad at Sara, but Sara forgot to tell your daughter she shouldn't sit next to Gabby because Allie had passed a note during science class that Brandon saw, which meant Brandon knew your daughter liked Jason, only Jason picked Amanda for a lab partner...!

Sometimes the best communication skill is to listen, then ask a non-threatening question such as "Then what happened?" With Sondra, I'll often smile and say, "Give me more details!" She happily obliges by going into great detail about the situation. If the topic is something upsetting, just letting her talk usually ends with her saying, "That's it. Thanks, Mom, for helping me out." In reality, I've simply listened, totally unable to keep track of all the details of who did what to whom while wearing what outfit. She simply needed me to listen.

Alexi, a 10-year old told us, "My mom says she wants to know about my day. When I start to tell her something, she interrupts. Then she gives all this advice. I don't like telling her what happened at school because she butts in and takes over." It's oh-so-hard to simply let our daughters talk without giving our expert opinion. Remember the root beer float analogy? Sometimes moms are a tiny scoop of ice cream while our daughters take over the majority of the glass as the root beer. As tweens talk, they often clarify and organize their thoughts. This helps them learn problem-solving skills.

When it comes to communicating, why is it that adults continue talking on their cell phones when they could be listening to their daughters? Of course, situations come up where business or important calls come through. Most times, though, cell phone calls are simply chitchat that can take place at other times.

Has this ever happened to you?

Mom (picking up daughter after school): "Hi, Candace. How was your day?"
Candace: "Mom, you won't believe what happened...."
(Ringing—or rather, the soundtrack from *Rocky*—comes from Mom's cell phone.)
Mom: "Hello? Hi, Linda! Oh, I know what you mean ... that bakery sells the best pies. Have you tried their pumpkin scones?" (Mom continues her conversation, oblivious to her daughter. After finishing the call, she looks over at Candace.) "Were you going to say something?"
Candace: "Never mind!"
End of conversation.

Since this chapter is about repeating yourself, I'll repeat the steps to developing effective communication with your daughter:

1. Say it once, and follow through.

2. Speak in shorter sentences.

3. Use notes to communicate.

4. Talk less, listen more.

5. Turn off the cell phone!

Just for Fun

Start a new tradition with your daughter. Talk (or communicate!) with her about a fun tradition the two of you or your entire family can do that no other family does. Here's what a mom with four kids did to add a fun tradition to her family.

"I know many families have very traditional traditions like serving Grandma's special cranberry-marshmallow salad each Thanksgiving. Our family is a little on the unconventional side, so we create our own traditions that are a bit off-the-wall. Whenever there's a full moon, we go outside and howl like wolves. (The neighbors are used to it!) When someone has a birthday, all the family members wake up the birthday person by forming a marching band. We use pots and pans to bang and march around the bedroom. Our kids have developed a real sense of humor by seeing its okay to have fun on a regular basis. They'll actually talk to us to help plan when the next wolf howl or birthday march will take place."

Chapter 4

Yes, Mom, I Would Jump Off a Bridge If My Friends Did

Remember how your daughter idolized you when she was 4? She'd race toward you after preschool, delighted to be together after a three-hour separation. Her face would light up with joy when you suggested a trip to the store for milk. At library story time, she'd snuggle her tiny body next to yours, content just to bask in your presence!

Now as a tween, it's hard to get as much as a subtle wave as you drop her off at school.

Brenda Nixon, a parenting author of *Parenting Power in the Early Years*, has this to say about tweens breaking away from their mothers and bonding with friends.

Pray, pray, pray and then distance yourself emotionally. Don't let every hormonal swing and fickleness influence your motherly response. Remember you're the adult and need to be stable. Sometimes girls say and do things that, more often than not, aren't meant as an attack. Repeat this phrase: "My daughter doesn't do things against me. She does things to meet her own needs."

Moms, stand strong! In spite of how your daughter treats you, you are still crucially important in her life. In a survey of girls age 12–18 conducted by Harris Interactive on behalf of the Gillette Company, nearly half of all respondents (48 percent) chose their own mothers as the best examples of "inner beauty." (Second choice Reese Witherspoon scored 26 percent, and Britney Spears ranked last among six choices, with 4 percent.)

The online survey also showed that mothers and friends scored high as sources of trusted advice: 46 percent of respondents chose their moms and

40 percent chose their friends; only 4 percent said that they thought a celebrity like Drew Barrymore would provide good advice.

When Sondra and I surveyed tween girls and their mothers, the surveys overwhelmingly placed mothers as the go-to person for advice. Alexis, a teenager in Nashville, wrote, "My mom and I will talk, but if it's too hard to talk about, then we would write notes back and forth through e-mails." Most girls, when asked who they go to when they have a problem, simply wrote, "My mom." One girl wrote, "I ALWAYS go to my mom!"

Moms, according to our survey, cherish time spent with their daughters.

> *Joyce, a graphic artist and mother of two teen daughters:* "The best thing about my daughters is enjoying my daughters as young ladies. Watching them grow has been a true pleasure for me. Having fun with music and singing. Dancing with them also, just really getting to know who they are. The giggles, the goofy times, the dressing up, the joy of seeing her succeed in whatever she does. The knowing that my daughters love me!"

So with all that positive information about warm, loving, mother-daughter relationships, it's time to transition to ... friends! Much as you want to be the center of your daughter's life, the tween years are a time when friends play an increasingly important role. You're no longer arranging play dates for your 5-year-old so she can learn socialization skills. Your 10-year-old confidently knows which friends she wants to spend time with, and she plans her own social activities.

Developmentally, it's important for your daughter to expand her world by spending time with friends. Most tweens have more freedom than in early childhood. Your daughter may take a different school bus home to be with a friend. This gives her confidence in new situations. Your daughter's friends help her figure out who she is. Should she dress preppy and fit in with the cool kids? What if she wants to join the chess club—does that make her a geek? As your daughter hangs out with friends, she's likely to evaluate who she is. Does she really like being a cheerleader? Would she be happier getting involved in gymnastics? Your daughter ventures out from within the security of her friends. Frustrating as it is to adults, your daughter learns about friendship from all the pathos and drama that goes on among tween girls. One day she's best friends with Caitlyn, and the next day your daughter wants to change schools to avoid seeing Caitlyn ever again.

Amy, a 15-year-old that answered our survey, was asked, "What's the best thing about being a young teenager?" She responded, "Being so close to your friends and having that bond." Let's look at some developmental reasons tweens find friends so important.

Consider all the physical changes your daughter is going through. Some girls have a 3½-inch growth spurt in one year. Not only are their pants getting shorter, but secondary sex characteristics are starting to develop. At the older end of the tween spectrum, girls start to develop body fat, acne, and body odor! That's an awful lot to handle when you're 13 years old. Sometimes it's easier to share with a friend going through the same thing than to talk with your mom.

You may wonder why your daughter has mood swings or trouble controlling her emotions. Just as a baby is learning to coordinate words with objects and physical development, your daughter is trying to coordinate her brain. (She just doesn't know it.) Studies show that connections between neurons are still incomplete at that age. In other words, your daughter needs support from her friends! An 11-year-old told us, "Sometimes I want to cry for no reason at all. It's silly because my day is going fine. I didn't fight with my mom, yet I want to cry. When I told my best friend, she said she cried at gymnastics yesterday ... and she didn't know why." As we all know, misery loves company, so tweens need their friends for moral support. After all, don't you call a friend when your regular hair stylist botches your haircut?

Which of the following situations helps your daughter more?

Mom: "Kelly, you seem quiet. Is something wrong?"
Kelly: "Nothing's wrong."
Mom: "Want to talk about it?"
Kelly: "I told you, nothing's wrong! It's just that stupid Jennie said I was a Goody Two-shoes because I got good grades. I'll flunk my math test. That will show her."
Mom: "Kelly, there's nothing wrong with getting good grades. You're a smart girl, and it's important to get good grades so you can go to college. Don't worry about what Jennie says. ...."

By this time, Kelly has tuned her mother out and is simply wallowing in the misery of being called a Goody Two-shoes. Contrast that dialogue with this one between Kelly and her friend Mollie.

Kelly: "I'm so mad! Do you know what that stupid Jennie said to me? She said I was a Goody Two-shoes!"
Mollie: "She's always so horrible! I can't stand her either. Last week she called me 'teacher's pet' because I offered to sort the spelling and English homework. She's mad because she had to stay in at recess and finish her work. I wish she'd transfer to another class!"
Kelly: "I wish she'd transfer to another school!"
Mollie: "Yeah, that would be great. School would be so much fun if she wasn't here."

With that, Kelly and Mollie walk off, ready to join their friends at lunch. Jennie is still an irritant, but Mollie and Kelly have gained confidence from each other, knowing they're united in their feelings toward Jennie.

Sometimes a mother's profound advice just can't compare to that of another 11-year-old!

Sammy, a 12-year-old, told us: "My mom's okay, but I can't tell her everything. She just doesn't understand what it's like to be in middle school. The classes are hard. Some teachers are mean. I need my friends for support, not my mom." Sammy's right. Our memories are vague about middle school angst. (Remember when it was called junior high?) Our role is to keep the lines of communication open, knowing that at times our daughters will confide in their friends.

Back to our root beer float analogy. As you put ice cream in your glass, you're trying to get a good combination of ice cream and root beer. Seven-eighths of a glass of root beer with a dollop of ice cream isn't the right combination. As moms, we're usually the seven-eighths glass full of root beer. We're a bit overbearing with our well-meaning advice and lectures. Your daughter's friends, however, provide a more balanced combination of root beer and ice cream. They help your daughter find "balance" in her life. You provide sound advice. Her friends give her a combination of fun, reality, and being kindred spirits.

Along with needing friends for support, a tween needs friends to help establish her identity. By "trying out" different friendships, your daughter starts making practical decisions about her own personality and interests. Your 9-year-old might be thrilled to hang out with like-minded horse lovers at the stables. A few years later, when many of these girls abandon horses for an interest in boys, your daughter and one close friend might decide to continue their interest in horses and try barrel racing or dressage. If your daughter's friends are supportive of her decision to stay in the horse world, she'll probably follow her heart and keep on riding.

Thirteen-year-old Gracie told us, "I love ballet class. All my friends and me took classes together up through fourth grade. Then my friends decided to go out for soccer. I hate dirt and running and those ugly soccer shorts. It was a hard decision, but I stayed with my dance classes. Now my friends come to my recitals and I sometimes go to their soccer games." Having a supportive group of friends helped Gracie establish that she's a budding ballerina rather than a future Mia Hamm.

Have you ever thought that your daughter's friends can be a positive influence on her? Girls are quick to point out unacceptable behavior. The following is not the most pleasant example, but it makes the point.

A mother had difficulty with her 9-year-old picking her nose in public. Mom's admonishments didn't do any good. Then one day her daughter and a friend were bowling. As her daughter unconsciously picked her nose, the other 9-year-old squealed, "Oh Callie! That is so *gross!* I'm never bowling with you again if you pick your nose!" That ended Callie's nose picking right then and there.

At this age, girls tell "the truth" because they don't have the skills to be tactful. Your daughter may come home in tears because little Melissa said your daughter was a lousy speller. More than likely, Melissa is right, even though there are more subtle ways to convey the information. Friends are a great opportunity for your daughter to develop a give-and-take relationship with peers.

While it's important that your daughter have friends, it's even more important *you* know her friends. Hillary Clinton is right: It does take a village to raise a child. The more communication parents have, the less likely tweens will get in trouble. Don't hesitate to call or meet your daughter's friends.

We recently moved across country to a new community. Sondra would come home and tell me she's going skating with Chloe or Amanda or Ashley. I, of course, had no idea who these girls were. So I called their parents to introduce myself, and every mom said something like, "Thanks for calling. It's so nice to have a mom interested in what their daughter is doing." When Sondra was in sixth grade, she made new friends at middle school. In order to get to know their mothers, we planned an afternoon craft party. I had simple refreshments set out, along with an assortment of craft projects. Eight moms and their daughters showed up for a casual afternoon where the girls had fun and the moms got to know each other. I felt much safer letting Sondra spend the night or go someplace with a friend after meeting her mom.

Sondra says: This was a really great idea that my mom had. At times I'd get frustrated when my mom wanted to call my friend's mothers. I know it simply meant my mom was concerned, but it still was annoying. After the craft party, the moms knew each other, and then it was so much easier to visit my friends. The moms felt comfortable with each other. It was also great for me to see that, even though my friends complained about how they didn't get along with their moms, in reality they got along just like my mom and I did. After we had this craft party, we didn't talk about how much our moms annoyed us any more. (Well, not quite as much!)

Mother-Daughter Mini-Activity

The next time you are at the store with your tween, let her pick out a small, blank notebook. Begin by taking the notebook and writing a short paragraph to your daughter. It could be congratulating her on a great report card or commenting on how proud you are that she helped her little brother with a school project. Put the notebook on her bed. Suggest that your tween read your message and then write a few sentences and put the notebook on your bed. Keep the process casual. You don't have to exchange the notebook on a daily basis. In most cases, tweens start to open up and write things they wouldn't tell you face-to-face. You'll find out about her friends, as well. The notebooks are also a wonderful way to have a record of your daughter's development—in handwriting, spelling, dealing with growing-up issues, and more.

Speaking of growing-up issues, Sondra, at 17, recently started dating. Naturally we'd much rather have her home with us playing Boggle, but we're making the best of the situation. (To save the poor boy embarrassment, we'll call him "Riley.") I knew Riley from school events and saw he was a respectful, fun kid. However, after he asked Sondra out on an official date, I needed to know more. When he arrived to pick up our precious daughter, I greeted him at the door, clipboard in hand.

"Hi, Riley," I said warmly. "Nice to see you. Before you go out with my daughter, I'd like to ask you a few questions."

Sondra, knowing our untraditional parenting techniques, just gave Riley a smile and said, "Welcome to my world!"

With that, we all sat down and I asked the nervous 18-year-old my first question. "Riley, tell me about your favorite ride at an amusement park."

Riley looked shocked, then relieved, then back to shock. "Is this a trick question?" he asked.

I assured him it wasn't and for the next 10 minutes we had a casual time getting to know him. He answered such thought-provoking questions as:

- If you had to cook for yourself, what could you make?
- What's the best Valentine's Day present you ever gave your mom?
- What teacher has had the biggest impact on your life?
- What's the most boring sermon you've ever heard?
- What are three rules of safe driving?

I wanted to ask, "What do you think will happen to you if you harm my daughter?" but my husband overruled me. He wanted to make sure Riley wasn't permanently traumatized by my questions.

As my daughter left with Riley, I felt comfortable, knowing he had given solid answers to my questions. More importantly, he had a relaxed attitude toward the whole unexpected interview process.

Sondra says: Luckily, my parents didn't scare Riley off. We sure laughed about the whole situation when we got into the car. When my parents came out with the clipboard, I was worried. I never quite know what my parents are about to do, or what they are capable of. The fact that they took this lighthearted approach let me know that they care about me. The second time he came over, my mom was preparing for a team-building keynote speech, and she was working out a new game that involved one person throwing celery at another person, who was holding scissors. The object was to cut the celery in the air with the open scissors. (Yes, this is the kind of activities we really do at our house!) Riley happened to come over at the moment where my mother was throwing celery at me. Well, needless to say, within seconds he had the scissors thrust into his hands so he could cut celery. It helped me know as well that he can take anything thrown at him—literally. Although I might roll my eyes at the crazy antics my parents do, they are great memories which I can look back on and laugh at.

Hopefully your tween daughters aren't dating yet. But when the time comes, feel free to use my questions to conduct your own pre-date interview! Sondra also handled the situation well, partly because of her outgoing personality. But what do you do when your daughter isn't so outgoing?

> *Carolyn, mom to a 13-year-old:* "My daughter has always been shy, but it's worse in middle school. No one picks on her. It's more like kids ignore her. I encourage her to invite someone over, but she's happy coming home and writing in her journal or playing with the dog. I wish she had more friends."

It's difficult watching a shy child stay at home when she could be having fun with friends. According to research, around 15 to 20 percent of children are born with a temperament that makes them shy, withdrawn, or timid. This isn't necessarily bad. After all, those of us with loud, outgoing (some might say, obnoxious) personalities need other people to laugh at our antics. Shyness isn't a problem unless it's at the stage where your daughter is scared to participate in class or refuses to try any new experience, such as skiing or going to camp. For most shy girls, timid behavior diminishes as self-confidence increases. Here are a few ways to help your daughter slowly break out of her shy personality.

- Avoid introducing your daughter as bashful, as in: "This is Jeff, my little athlete. And this is Michaela, our shy child." With an introduction like that, do you expect Michaela to do a Bette Midler imitation and announce, "Yes, I'm Michaela, and I'm great! Want to hear me sing the 'Star Spangled Banner' while twirling my baton?"
- Continue exposing your daughter to new, nonthreatening experiences. Take her to the Easter breakfast at Grandma's retirement center or to an outdoor concert. Simply say, "Sometimes in new situations, its fine to simply look around and observe what's going on." You don't need to force your daughter to audition for the school play, but she should attend a performance and support her sister in the role of the Yellow Brick in an adapted version of *The Wizard of Oz.*
- Role-play new situations with your daughter so she knows what to expect. Act out what it's like to get on an airplane and have the flight attendant ask if she wants a minuscule package of gourmet peanuts. Practice two or three things to say when Aunt Edna comes to visit. Some girls need specific skills to help them get through stressful situations.
- Teach your daughter how to handle basic social situations. What should she say when she meets your boss at a company picnic and the boss says, "Hi, Annie. How are you?" If your daughter is swinging at the park and a classmate from school says, "Hey, Shannon! Want to go down the slide with me?" what can she say?

When Sondra was a preschooler, we taught her to answer questions "with lots of words." (Later, we taught her to "answer in full sentences.")

For example, if someone asked her how old she was, a typical answer might be, "I'm four," but we taught her to say, "I'm four years old and my birthday is in November." This gives the other person more information to continue the conversation. (They also usually commented on what a bright child she was, which reinforced her longer answers.) As she got older, Sondra quickly saw that speaking in full sentences resulted in adults giving her positive feedback.

Let's compare these two conversations:

Librarian: "Hi, Sondra. Going to check out some books today?"
Sondra: "Yes."
Librarian: "We have some new books about castles on the display table."
Sondra: "Thanks."

Nothing wrong with that conversation. Yet, by encouraging Sondra to speak in full sentences, the conversation went like this:

Librarian: "Hi, Sondra. Going to check out some books today?"
Sondra: "Yes, I think I want another book about castles. I like the one you showed me last week."
Librarian: "I'm so glad you liked it. What was your favorite part?"
Sondra: "I liked where they gave the directions for how to make your own castle. My dad and I collected boxes and toilet paper rolls and made the coolest castle. I sprinkled it with glitter, too."
Librarian: "What fun! There's a new book about castles on the display table. It has lots of color pictures."
Sondra: "Thanks! I'll let you know how I liked it next week."
(As Sondra walks away, she overhears the librarian tell me, "Your daughter is so much fun to talk with!")

I recently heard about an inner-city school where the children were taught a set reply for whenever someone asked, "What's your name?" Their answer was a variation on, "My name is Sarah, and I'll be starting college in 2012." Now that's a way to build self-confidence!

With a shy child, look for tiny steps to progress. If your child greets an unfamiliar relative with eye contact, a smile, and a "hello," compliment her. Let her know you noticed the effort she made to smile at Uncle Howard. She'll gain confidence because you acknowledged her actions in a positive way.

Here's a true confession on my part. Our older daughter Trina was a perfect child to a certain extent. She simply did everything "right." This girl didn't need to be reminded to do homework. She was respectful, completed her chores, and wrote thank-you notes for birthday presents. A mother's dream? Not in my case. I wanted a daughter with spunk, willing to push right to the limits. Trina never got grounded, because she didn't do anything wrong.

When she was a sophomore in high school, I told her, "Trina, I want you to know what it feels like to break a rule. Before you graduate in two years, I want you to skip at least one class. You need to experience the feeling of having your heart pound and your palms sweat because you might get caught." My poor daughter was horrified, but in true Trina fashion, agreed to my request.

At the end of Trina's junior year, I got a phone call midday. In a muffled voice, she said, "Mom, I did it. I skipped science class. What should I do now?" I suggested she go to the library, knowing she'd be traumatized if I told her to leave campus. That evening, she gave us a detailed explanation of her big adventure (which paled in comparison to my high school escapade of breaking into an amusement park at night and crawling up the roller coaster tracks with my friends). Most of all, she worried about getting back into science class without a pass. I reassured her that, with her record, the teacher would let her into class, never imagining that she had skipped. Fortunately, I was right, and she survived the experience with little psychological damage. She is quick to point out to others that her mother encouraged her to skip school!

Whether your daughter is shy or outgoing, friends play an important part in her life. But what happens when you don't approve of your daughter's friends?

> *Linda, a teacher and the mother of two teens:* "If I had the chance to raise my daughters again, I'd pay more attention to who they hung out with. I was spineless in not saying no when I didn't feel comfortable with their friends. I did have control. I just didn't use it."

Have you ever had your daughter's friend come over and felt uncomfortable with the girl's behavior? Sondra had a friend in sixth grade that would never look directly at me (we'll call her "Emma"). Emma wasn't shy, but she gave me the feeling she was hiding something. When I served an after-school snack in the kitchen, she wanted to eat upstairs. If I suggested the girls play outside where I could see them, she encouraged Sondra to stay in the rec room. She seldom smiled or said please or thank you. One day, I found a purse in the street by our house. Opening it up to find the owner's identification, I saw that it belonged to Emma's mom. The purse also contained $600 cash! Naturally, I called Emma's mom—who picked up the purse without even saying thank you. It confirmed my feelings that Sondra's relationship with Emma needed to be monitored.

Ann Landers once gave some terrific advice to a mother complaining about her daughter's choice of friends. The newspaper columnist said, "Try not to say anything negative about your daughter's friend. The minute you point out the friend's lack of manners or bad habits, you're daughter feels obligated to defend her friend." That makes sense. Remember when you were dating and your mom asked, "When is Steven getting a haircut?" Even if you thought Steven's hair *was* a bit shaggy, you'd give a passionate speech about how much you like his hair, ending with a dramatic "You never like any of my friends!"

Let's listen to a newspaper advice columnist and do our best not to openly criticize our daughters' friends. It's helpful if your daughter has several friends to choose from. That way you can gently guide her towards positive, upbeat friends. Encourage her to make friends with a wide range of girls. There's nothing wrong with becoming friends with girls from different backgrounds, income levels, and cultures, as long as they have the same basic principles as your family.

With your daughter, brainstorm a list of ways to make friends. This is not meant to win the popularity contest at school, but is simply a way to help her expand her range of friendships. When Sondra was in fourth grade, she became friends with a girl with a serious blood disease. Every few weeks, the girl had to spend a few hours getting a complete blood transfusion. Sondra developed a whole new appreciation for a friend that couldn't be as physically active as she was.

Here are some tips on making friends to add to the list you and your daughter develop:

- Take an interest in other people. If a girl at school says, "Yesterday I had to get a tooth pulled at the dentist," resist the urge to tell her about your last dentist appointment. Instead, ask what happened, how she feels now, and so on.
- Let your personality come through. If you're outgoing, get kids excited about the first sixth-grade basketball game of the season. If you like writing poetry, invite someone to join the after-school writing club.
- Participate in a few activities. Join the Girl Scouts or sign up for a swim team. You'll meet people with the same interests.
- Think how a new kid feels at school. Even if you feel awkward, go up and introduce yourself. Offer to show her where the bathroom is or how to check out a book at the library.
- Smile at people! It's so easy, and people respond to a friendly face.

Sondra says: One time when I was in middle school, my mom challenged me to not talk about myself for a day. Being the naturally confident preteen I was, I boldly accepted the task and didn't think it would be a problem. I remember just how hard it was to not tell my perfectly relevant story in history class. We were talking about Gettysburg, and I wanted to share about our visit there. When my friends talked about getting sick, I wanted to tell my graphic story of getting food poisoning. It was a real challenge not to talk about myself. Obviously I know there is a time and place where it's appropriate to talk about yourself. Even today, I try to resist telling *all* my great stories or adding *every* one of my anecdotes. It amazes me when I go back and look at my yearbooks, how many people wrote, "You're such a great listener." It wasn't that I was a good listener. I just let them talk, rather them making it all about me.

Looking for information on how to peel a pineapple, fix a leaky faucet, or deal with your tween's mood swings? Check out the hundreds of websites at www.about.com. They have "experts" on any possible topic. For example, look up www.parentingteens.about.com for helpful articles and advice from professionals on dealing with tweens.

Just for Fun

The next time your daughter has friends over, let them make a Kitty Litter Cake! (Don't worry—it's not as bad as it sounds!) The directions are simple:

1. Have the girls make a 9-inch by 13-inch rectangular sheet cake from a packaged mix.
2. Let it cool, and then frost with vanilla frosting.
3. Sprinkle a thin layer of Grape-Nuts cereal over the top to look like kitty litter.
4. Here's where realism comes in. Unwrap four or five miniature Tootsie Rolls and place them in the microwave for 6–8 seconds to get them soft. Are you ready for the next step? "Pinch" the ends of the Tootsie Rolls to look like ... well, to look like cat poop! Place the Tootsie Rolls on top of the Grape-Nuts.
5. To really carry out the kitty litter theme, buy a new kitty litter scoop and use it to slice the pieces of cake! Serve with root beer floats, of course!

Tweens get a kick out of making this cake. They might want to take it to school and gross out their teachers.

Chapter 5

Help! My Tween Won't Talk to Me!

During the early tween years, when your daughter is 9 or 10, you're still her greatest confidante. She'll tell you about the fire drill they had at school, and how Jacob was in the bathroom and didn't know where the class went so he got upset, and then Lindsey tripped and cut her knee so she had to find the nurse, but the nurse was outside so Mrs. Johnson gave Lindsey a Band-Aid, but the fire alarm was so loud it scared the kindergartners and they were crying, so Mrs. Johnson had to leave Lindsey, and then the fire alarm stopped but everyone was outside, so the principal said they could have an unscheduled recess, so your daughter ran to the slides, and ... ! You are in-the-know about the daily escapades of fourth-grade life!

Now fast-forward a few years, and you find your daughter a bit more reluctant to open up. When asked about her day, she'll give you a token amount of information such as, "We had an assembly about Martin Luther King Jr. Day." (Some mothers are happy to get that much information!) Naturally, as mothers, we still want to know every nuance of our daughter's life. (Well, maybe just most nuances!)

> *Susan, whose daughter just turned 13:* "I miss our bedtime chats. We used to have these great conversations as I tucked her into bed. Now she won't even let me kiss her goodnight! How can I keep the lines of communication open with my daughter?"

As with most things, "This too shall pass." Many mothers report they find themselves in a wonderful newfound relationship as their daughters are 18 and heading off to college. Their sullen teen suddenly transforms into a vibrant young woman, openly communicating with Mom. One solution, then, is to send your tween daughter to boarding school until she's 18. Or, you could work on communicating with your daughter, using various mom-tested ideas.

One mother wrote in her survey:

> "When my daughter began sharing less and less of her life, I begged. Yes, I begged and told her my life was full of stress as an accountant and asked her to humor me by having a five-minute talk with me every day. We'd actually set the timer, have a decent conversation for 300 seconds, and then she'd leave. Pretty soon the conversations got longer and she'd disregard the timer's bell. Sometimes she'd laugh and ask if I wanted two five-minute sessions of conversation."

That may seem like a "formal" solution, but it's certainly worth a try. Bring out the timer and see how much communication is possible in five minutes. Groveling never hurts!

In the business world, all companies at one time or another offer training in communication skills. I know—I often *present* those workshops to employees who would rather clean the company toilets than endure another communication workshop. Instead of making you sit through a two-hour presentation of "The Art of Effective Communication," I'll give you one highlight of my verbal presentation in the form of easy reading.

In speaking to adults, one important aspect of communication involves asking open and closed questions. Here's how it works with tweens. Many moms try to start a conversation with their daughters by asking a closed question—a question that basically requires a one- or two-word answer. It usually goes like this:

Mom: "How was school?"
Lizzie: "Okay."
Mom: "Do you have any homework?"
Lizzie: "A little."
Mom: "Did you still have a substitute in math class?"
Lizzie: "Yeah."

Thrilling conversation, isn't it? Now try the same conversation using an open-ended question that requires more than a yes-or-no answer.

Mom: "Anything funny happen at lunch today?"
Lizzie: "Oh, Mom, it was so gross. Brandon was eating chicken noodle soup and started laughing at Caleb's joke and noodles came out his nose!"
Mom: "What was the funny joke? I could use a good laugh."
Lizzie: "I didn't even hear the joke. I just saw Brandon snorting, then his face got red and then noodles come came out his nose."

Mom: "Sure beats eating in the staff lunchroom like I did. You had a substitute teacher in math yesterday. Why has Mrs. Taylor been gone for three days?"

Lizzie: "I think she's got some sort of flu. She's supposed to be back on Wednesday."

Look at that. Just by asking open-ended questions, you get graphic descriptions of noodles coming out of a 12-year-old's nose. What better form of communication can you want? There's no guarantee you'll get lengthy conversation from your daughter by asking open-ended questions, but you do stand a better chance of having her talk to you with more words than "yeah" or "no." After a while, those open-ended questions lead to deeper conversations about poor grades or problems with friends.

While your daughter can't bring herself to tell you, she's probably glad to have a chance to let you know what's going on in her life, even if it involves recycled noodles. Ella, an 11-year-old, wrote on her survey: "I wish I could tell my mom what's happening in my life. She just asks if I have homework and tells me to do it. Or she tells me to do my chores. I don't like her giving me orders all the time." Open-ended questions give your daughter the open-ended opportunity to share her thoughts and feelings.

If Sondra's involved in a play, she frequently has drama rehearsal until 9:30 or 10:00 PM. We try to stay up to say goodnight to her, and this has developed into quite a communication ritual. Allan and I are usually reading in bed. Sondra, still keyed up from rehearsal, opens our door and yells, "I'm home!" Then she takes a diving leap onto our bed. I know what's about to happen, so I quietly move to one side. She lies on her back between us and starts moving her arms and legs as if she's making a snow angel, saying, "Can't I get a little more room?' Allan refuses to budge, so the two of them jostle for more room on the bed. He's at a disadvantage, being under the covers and unable to move. Sondra usually manages to push him off the bed. (Yes, the blankets and pillows by this time are all over the floor.) Allan gets back under the blankets, and Sondra, once again between us, says with a smirk, "Okay, go ahead and ask me some open-ended questions." So we ask about a sick friend, a cranky teacher, or an upcoming term paper. We ask questions; she gives us detailed answers. Maybe not the most traditional communication situation, but it keeps us up-to-date on what's happening in her life.

Many mothers find that communication occurs during casual times. "I've asked my daughter to help me with my exercise plan," said a mother of a 13-year-old. "She's agreed to go to the Y with me twice a week. We have time together on the drive over, and then we talk while walking on the indoor track. It's much easier for her to open up when there isn't direct eye contact. Plus, I've lost five pounds!" How's that for a new weight-loss plan?

> *Mary, mother of an 11-year-old:* "I still lie down with my daughter after she gets in bed, and with the lights off, this gives her a chance to talk about whatever is on her mind, what happened at school, her friends, her classes, just anything at all. Often as I am leaving, she will say, 'Mama, tell me something to dream about so I will have good dreams.' This helps keep our relationship positive."

Before Sondra got her license and began zipping all over town in her bright yellow VW Bug, I found driving her friends to different events was a great way to eavesdrop in a politically correct way. Could I help it if I overheard that Michelle had a crush on Jordan? Later, when everyone was dropped off, I would casually ask Sondra what she thought of Michelle and Jordan's relationship. Face it—tweens know their mothers listen in on car conversations. It's an understood tween rule that if you really don't want the adult driver to hear something, the topic is never discussed.

Another mother shared an unusual way she communicated with her children. The family owns a working dishwasher, she said, but seldom uses it.

> "We have a rotating schedule where one night a week I wash and dry dishes by hand with one of my three children. It's a time for the two of us to be together in a casual way, which opens up communication. Plus, none of my other kids ever interrupt because they're worried they'll have to help!"

Whether conversing with your daughter in the car, on the YMCA track, or while washing dishes, a few rules apply to all situations. In order to encourage positive communication, remember these tips:

• Much as you want to share your years of profound wisdom, try to avoid lecturing. If your daughter tells you she's thinking of piercing her nose, stifle the urge to scream and lecture her on the dangers of piercing various body parts. Besides, she'll just tell you that you both have pierced ears, so what's wrong with a pierced nose? Give her a silent lecture in your mind. Let her talk, while you listen and ask a few appropriate open-ended questions. Bethany, an 11-year-old, told us: "I'm scared to talk to my mom about some things. She'll start going on and on with some lecture that doesn't even make sense. I'm not even done talking and she's already lecturing me."

• Unless you're driving, give your daughter your undivided attention if she's trying to talk to you about a serious issue. That means not checking the mail or answering your cell phone. If you're serious about communicating with your daughter, let her know she has your focus. Naturally, times occur when you're making dinner and she's chatting about the pros and cons of cooked carrots versus raw carrots. In that case, continue what you're doing with as much eye contact as possible.

Sondra says: I certainly don't have to worry about my mom talking on the cell phone when I'm with her. She doesn't use a cell phone! Yes, my mother is probably the only mom in the U.S. that doesn't have a cell phone in her purse. (Actually, my mom doesn't even carry a purse, but that's another story.) I've learned that if I can't reach my mom at home, there's not much I can do. She claims she raised my older sister Trina without a cell phone, so there's no reason I won't survive without being in constant contact with her.

• Sometimes facts help you make a point. If your daughter wants to start dating at 12 ... let her. (Not really!) After listening to her and giving your opinion, do a little homework of your own. Find a short article or a few paragraphs in a book showing the risks associated with dating at a young age. Maybe, just maybe, your daughter will pay attention to an outside source rather than her mother.

Sondra says: My mom always cuts out magazine and newspaper articles for me and has them lying on my plate when I come down to breakfast in the morning. My mother feels that I should go to bed when she does (at the unreasonable hour of 9:30!). So she put an article on my plate describing research on how teen weight gain was connected to loss of sleep. The next night, I didn't go to bed at my usual 12:30, but got into bed at 11:30 instead. Not quite the ultimate goal of my mother, but it was something.

She doesn't always put articles that relate just to my life. Many times she will put interesting articles about something going on in the world that I had no clue was happening. I've found that now as I read the paper, I will see an article I think would interest one of my friends. I'll cut it out and put it in their locker or give it to them.

At times when I don't want to take in what my mom is saying, I'm better at accepting it from another source. The magazine articles help with that.

• While it's hard to admit, sometimes our daughters need privacy, not our questions, open-ended or otherwise. Let your daughter know you're available to listen if she wants to talk. Often, just a few days (or hours) of feeling she's in control of her life will help her open up. She needs time to process a problem or situation on her own. Knowing you're available gives her the freedom to talk when she's ready.

Sondra says: School can be an emotional place. There are days when I just need to come home and process something before I can talk to my mom about it. I might even have to talk to a friend about something before I talk to my parents. It's nothing against them, but sometimes advice or even just a listening ear of a friend is more helpful than having my parents comfort me. Your daughter will come to you when she is ready. No matter how fickle my problem is (and as much as I hate to admit it), my mom's hug is always helpful.

• Don't argue about her feelings. When she says, "I feel like I don't have any friends," she's not asking you to tell her that Courtney, Allie, Marissa, and Emily are all her friends. She may have friends, but her feelings are also valid. Let her express her feelings. Then at a later time, help her put those feelings in perspective by sharing some facts. If she's struggling in math, it's true when she says she feels like "the most stupid person on the planet." After she's expressed her feelings, help her come up with a concrete plan of action. Can she get a tutor? Go in early and ask the teacher for help? Study extra hard? It's hard to disagree with a person's feelings. (Although tween feelings seem to fluctuate from one extreme to another!)

• If you feel your daughter has a serious topic to discuss but clams up around you, enlist another adult. Ask a favorite aunt or adult female friend to take your daughter out to breakfast. Sometimes your daughter needs the influence of another caring adult.

• Communication isn't always about words. A Jewish proverb says, "A mother understands what a child does not say." Sometimes a wink, a pat on the arm, or a thumbs-up conveys a message to your daughter. If she's feeling sad about not getting the lead in the school play, a quick hug will communicate your love better than any conversation about all the other plays she can audition for.

• Find creative ways to communicate with your daughter. An unexpected balloon bouquet with a card that reads, "I'm so glad you are my daughter," conveys love and caring.

Try some of these other communication activities:

1. Write positive statements about your tween and put them on her bathroom mirror or inside her math notebook.

2. Rent a movie you loved as a tween and watch it with your daughter. I admit, I had the original *Parent Trap* movie with Hayley Mills completely memorized. Sondra humors me by watching it, and then we sing "Let's Get Together" to each other. That's all I ask for as a mother.

3. Buy her an appropriate tween magazine for fun bedtime reading.

4. Smile when she walks into the room.

5. Plan a special after-school activity for the two of you.

6. Have spontaneous fun. Stop and buy hot fudge sundaes on the way home from violin lessons ... before dinner!

7. Toss a pillow at her as she walks by.

8. Get a joke book and tell her some corny knock-knock jokes.

9. Find the address of her favorite athlete or author and ask for an autographed picture.

10. Share a root beer float. Tell her the tiny bubbles that foam up when the root beer hits the ice cream reminds you of her bubbly personality.

11. If she's going to a sleepover camp, send a postcard a few days before she leaves. She'll be the only camper to have mail on the first day of camp.

12. If possible, take her out of school to go with you if you have an out-of-town business trip.

Sondra says: Many times when I've had less than a perfect day, a simple gesture from my mom can bring me out of my bad mood. I remember one time I was feeling bad about math class. After studying really hard, my grade didn't reflect my work. My mom gave me a skirt she thought I would like that she had bought me, for no particular reason, while she was out shopping. (She's pretty cheap, so that's a big deal!) This simple gesture made me realize that she loves me no matter if I did do badly on a test. It made me forget about my bad grade and realize that there are more important things in life.

As you can see, communication means more than asking your daughter about her homework assignments. Some mothers find the whole communication process fairly easy. Dottie, the mother of an 18-year-old, was asked, "Now that your daughter is in high school, what would you have done differently with your daughter in the early teen years?" She gave simple but valuable advice: "Nothing different. We have always communicated together very well. We've worked at fostering this by setting routines of eating together and talking in the evenings when she was home." If it works for Dottie, it might work for you. Try eating together and setting a routine time for talking.

Mother-Daughter Mini-Activity

Try this idea as a way to keep the lines of communication open with your daughter. Get two large envelopes for you and your daughter and decorate them with stickers and markers. You want the envelopes to convey fun. Attach one envelope outside your bedroom and the other outside your daughter's. Try to make a habit of writing short notes to each other and leaving them in your respective paper mailboxes. Sometimes the notes can be a simple "I love you" or a request, such as, "I'm sorry I got upset with you this morning. Can we talk about it this evening?"

On a slightly different note, we found that many girls answering our surveys had had situations where they could benefit from communication with a sympathetic adult. When asked what they would change about their life, here are some answers:

- "I wish my daddy would get out of jail."
- "I wish my parents hadn't divorced when I was younger."
- "I wish I could change the way I look, because I think I look ugly."
- "I wish I could change a thing I did with a guy."
- "I wish I had a better life like if my Dad was there for me."

If you get the chance, try communicating with some of your daughter's friends. You may be just the caring adult they need in their life.

Just for Fun

Take your daughter to a scrapbook store, even if you're not crafty. Buy a scrapbook and some of those fancy papers and stickers and shiny ribbons that fanatic scrapbookers have. Spend a few days going through all your old photos and making a scrapbook depicting activities you two have done together. You'll end up with a treasured keepsake, plus have great communication talking about each picture. Be sure to repeat the story of your painful labor experience giving birth. Then tell her how the pain was worth it because she's such a wonderful daughter!

Sondra says: Scrapbooking or doing crafts with my mom is always a great chance to talk to her without feeling like I'm being scrutinized. Many times teens feel like they are talking to a shrink when they are just talking to their parent one-on-one. I know personally I am much more willing to open up and talk to my mother if there is something else going on. When I am the only focus of her attention, I feel uncomfortable. But when I don't have to make eye contact and can be doing something with my hands, it allows me to open up and tell her what's really going on in my life. Scrapbooking is also fun because you can recount all the memories you shared together. I love looking at old pictures with my mom and thinking about all the crazy things we have done. It helps to know that even though we might get into fights every once in a while, we have hundreds of good memories that far outweigh the bad ones!

Chapter 6

What Does She See
in Lindsay Lohan?

When you think about advertisers targeting tween girls, you envision seductive ads for Britney Spears perfume and thong underwear sold at Limited Too. Have you ever considered that the media is targeting your daughter in the form of air fresheners as well?

Get ready for these statistics: Total sales of air fresheners are expected to reach $1.72 billion in 2007, and more than a thousand new kinds of air fresheners hit the market in 2006. You're probably asking, "How do air fresheners relate to my 12-year-old?" (Even though the smell from her dirty socks permeates the entire house.) Answer: SC Johnson, which makes household products all of us use, has released a Glade air freshener specifically targeted toward tweens. The Scented Oil Light Show plugs into a wall and beams bright lights along with scents. Naturally the scents have tween-friendly names such as Berry Burst, Watermelon Rush, and Vanilla & Cream. There's even a Glade "Create-a-Scent" Plug-In, which lets tweens make their own scent combinations. You might have seen the commercial where a tween girl complains that her mother bought air freshener for her brother instead of her. The company is focusing on the buying power of tween girls. Evidently, tweens have quite the buying power, because the Glade Light Show costs $11.99. A Febreze "player" costs $27.49, and discs are $5.99 a piece. Whatever happened to those inexpensive pine tree air fresheners we all had hanging from our car mirrors?

Air fresheners seem like a relatively harmless item companies are targeting toward your young daughter. But what about the thousands of other, not so innocent messages your daughter receives from the media?

Advertisers suggest tweens who don't have the latest clothes, jewelry, makeup, and electronic products won't be popular. Tweens see seductive commercials on a constant basis, even before they understand what the seduction is about.

Sylvia Rimm, author of *Growing Up Too Fast*, conducted a study with 5,400 8- to 12-year-olds. She found that about 10–20 percent of the tweens perform sex acts they see in movies, have oral sex parties, experiment with drugs, are obsessed with body image, and drink beer and mixed drinks. Okay, after you've pulled yourself up off the floor, remember that it is still a small percentage of tweens participating in unhealthy behavior. Of course your daughter can be influenced by what she sees and hears, but hopefully, with your influence, she'll make the right choices with your guidance.

Here's the good news: once again, as mothers, we have the power to influence our daughters' behavior. Not 100 percent control, but enough to make a dramatic impact in their lives. Many experts agree that parents are being too lenient when it comes to how much they let the media influence their daughters. As Rimm puts it: "Parents are overpowering their kids, giving them too many choices. They don't see what kids without boundaries are like in high school" (1).

Speaking of choices, take a look at how the media are encouraging tweens to spend their money (or their parent's money!).

- The Brewster Wallcovering Company is selling a line of wallpapers specifically marketed toward tweens. The "Whizz Kids" collection offer a variety of patterns to fit any tween's personality.
- Victoria's Secret has a new department called "Pink," offering stuffed animals, sparkly pajama bottoms, and T-shirts with Pink's mascot, a pink dog. (Clever, isn't it?) Tweens regularly shop in the Pink department, even buying basic sweatpants at $68 each.
- Club Libby Lou has more than 80 retail locations. These stores feature in-store parties with themes such as Sparkle Princess, Drama Queen, and Trend Setter. Girls and their friends spend the afternoon getting glammed up with tiaras and makeup.
- Disney and Nickelodeon provide cell phone ringtones and content. Tic Talk and Firefly are two phones marketed as "starter phones" for young tweens.
- Sweet Georgia Brown, a tween-focused cosmetics company, sells body oils labeled "Follow the Boy" and "Vanilla Vibe."
- Sex Bracelets are a new tween fad. These soft plastic bracelets correlate a sex act with a specific color. Pink = kiss. Blue = blow job. White = lap dance. Boys come along and rip a bracelet off a girl's wrist. The girls are supposed to perform the act related to the color bracelet the boy is waving in front of her.
- The ever-popular Bratz dolls with plump lips and provocative outfits are marketed to 6- to 10-year-olds.

- Many spas now market treatments to young girls. It's not unusual to have 8-year-olds with highlighted hair and French manicures scheduling monthly mini-facials.

There's no denying our daughters are bombarded with sexually explicit ads from all directions. Now ask yourself this question: Do you *have to* buy your daughter a Bratz doll? Can she survive without a French manicure? How about having her birthday party at a roller rink instead of a store selling mini-thong underwear? In other words, moms do have power to control some of the media attracting our daughters.

"Kids wear sexually provocative clothes at nine because their parents buy them provocative clothes, not because of their hormones," explains Robert L. Johnson, director of adolescent and young-adult medicine at the University of Medicine and Dentistry of New Jersey.

Moms have control over the purse strings. Your daughter may get some birthday money from Grandma, but overall, we know who writes the check for those designer jeans. There's nothing wrong with telling your daughter the sequined T-shirt emblazed with "HOTT" isn't something you want her to wear.

Mother-Daughter Mini-Activity

Sit down with your daughter and some old magazines. Help her cut out a variety of fashions. Discuss each outfit and see if you can agree if the item is something you'd buy for your daughter. Glue the examples on a large piece of tag board labeled "Appropriate" and "Inappropriate." Before you go on your next shopping trip, remind your daughter to take a look at the appropriate outfits to help in her fashion selection.

Teachers complain of 10- or 11-year-old girls arriving at school looking like madams, in full cosmetic regalia with streaked hair, platform shoes, and midriff-revealing shirts. Lillian, a teacher speaking with parents at a school open house in Ohio, suggested parents set some standards when buying clothes for their daughters. Immediately she was bombarded by moms objecting, "But that's the fashion! My daughter would be so upset if she couldn't wear her lacy camisole."

I'm not suggesting you dress your 11-year-old in a smocked dress with white knee socks and Mary Janes. Girls can still be both fashionable and age appropriate.

Sondra says: I was at a weekend conference called "Girls of Grace." They had music and speakers, all geared to 11- to 16-year-old girls. I thought their fashion show had a great "twist." They selected girls from the audience to model a bunch of clothes. First, a girl would come out in a super-short jean skirt with a low-cut tank top that showed her stomach. The next girl modeled a similar, but more conservative, outfit. She had on a longer jean skirt and a T-shirt under the tank top. It still was fashionable, but not so revealing. It made the point that girls can wear cute clothes without showing so much skin!

After a presentation I gave at a conference in New York, a mother came up to me and said, "You know what the problem is with a lot of moms? They've forgotten that 'parent' is also a verb." Another mom chimed in, "That's right. It's like these parents think raising kids is an extracurricular activity. They squeeze parenting in between their work, friends, and going to the gym. I get so tired of moms wondering why their daughters know the lyrics to these sexually provocative songs. It's because moms aren't actively taking an interest in their kids!" Those moms certainly knew what they were talking about. *Parent* is an action word! We need to take action and limit the media's influence on our daughters.

> *Chelsea, age 11:* "My older brother is home when I get home from school. He's usually watching some TV or video that has lots of shooting and people getting their guts cut out. There's sex, too. I don't really like watching it, but there's not much else to do."

Many parenting experts are seeing a double whammy with this age group. The media promote sexiness to girls who are often home alone after school. Away from adult influences, girls watch TV and go on-line without supervision. Many parents feel comfortable leaving their tween daughters alone for a few hours after school. This gives them more time to communicate with their peers, who also are caught up in the media glitz of adult-inspired fashion and inappropriate videos.

Twelve-year-old Allie wrote: "My mom doesn't really care what I do after school. So I go to my friend's house and we look at *Cosmo* magazines and listen to music."

Stop!! Have you looked at *Cosmo* lately? Here are the titles on a recent cover:

• Naughty Sex: 8 Hot New Positions We've Never Before Published
• Below His Belt Bloopers
• The Sexiest Things to Do after Sex
• How to Keep Your Guy Totally Turned On by You

Can you see any reason that tweens should be reading *Cosmo*? Think what kind of images Allie is getting as she and her friends read this magazine.

If an adult can't be home after school, check out some after-school resources for your daughter. A study of the Better Educated Students for

Tomorrow (BEST) after-school program in Los Angeles found that sixth- through ninth-grade students who participated in an after-school program were less likely to drop out of high school, contributing to a 20 percent improvement in the district's dropout rate. Provide alternatives for your daughter so she doesn't have time to vegetate in front of the TV.

> *Eva Marie, an author and speaker:* "We let our daughter have too much access to the media. I never realized the impact of media until we were inundated with its effects. If I had any advice for mothers, it would be: Don't ask general questions. Ask detailed questions. Watch the amount of media they are exposed to."

Are you aware how much TV your daughter watches? Do you know what she's doing on the computer? You may think she's doing research for her report on the Amazon River, while in reality she's harassing someone on-line.

> *12-year-old Caitlin:* "I had a nasty encounter with a girl in fifth grade. I was 11 years old. This girl had been my friend when I was 8, but since then we had grown apart. This girl verbally abused me through AIM [AOL Instant Messenger]. She said bad things that I know she would have never said in person. She called me bad words; she made fun of me and even told me no one liked me! In fact, she tried to turn everyone against me. She told lies to our classmates, started rumors, and gave me a bad reputation. I reacted by begging for forgiveness and kissing up to her. I did not know what I had done wrong. In fact, I had not done anything wrong. She was just a mean girl. Finally, I decided to tell my parents. They talked to the other girl's parents and things calmed down a little. She apologized a few weeks later and told me she was competing with me for popularity. Three years later, we still remember the incident."

And what about pornography? Donna Rice Hughes, an internet safety advocate, said, "Parents must utilize safety rules and software tools.... One in four kids last year accidentally came across pornography on-line. This is because of deceptive marketing tactics used by online pornographers.... No law can take the place of good parenting. Latchkey kids are most vulnerable to sexual predators."

Magazines, television, instant messaging, computers, and even billboards all assault our daughters with negative messages. Once again, it's time for moms to take control and see what we can do to limit media's influence. According to the Pew Internet & American Life Project, 60 percent of teens have gotten an e-mail or instant message from a perfect stranger, and 63 percent of those who have gotten such e-mails or IMs say

they have responded to strangers on-line. See what you have to look forward to when your daughter grows up?

> *Lindsey, age 12:* "Sometimes it's creepy being home alone after school
> with just my dog. I get onto chat rooms because it feels good to write
> back and forth. It's like they care about me."

Extra Parenting Tip

Try some of these ideas to show your daughter you care about her.

- Put a note in her lunch bag
- Make cookies together
- Occasionally put fresh flowers in her room
- Take a class or learn a skill like CPR together
- Ask her to explain why she likes a particular song
- Do a craft project together
- Go for a walk together
- Greet her with a cheerful "Good morning" even if you haven't had your coffee
- Share a joke or cartoon
- Casually touch her as you walk by or pass in the hall
- Say "I'm proud of you for _____"
- Let her overhear you praising her to a friend or relative
- Tell her "I love you" daily

Now back to the nitty-gritty of controlling the media's influence on your
daughter.

Positive media do exist! American Girl, in addition to dolls, offers
books, craft kits, and cooking activities, all geared toward tweens. When
Sondra was nine, we read the books out loud to each other, crying when
Addie was reunited with her dad and struggling with Kirsten as she
adjusted to America. The company's magazine is filled with quizzes,
articles on pets, and other age-appropriate activities. Check out the website at www.americangirl.com for more information about their movies
and computer games. You can feel confident your daughter won't get any
tips on French kissing!

Sondra says: One summer, when I was 10, we bought an American Girl theater
kit. It had all the scripts and directions to put on a play about Samantha. I gave
my friends their parts ahead of time to memorize. (I had the lead, of course!) We

set a Saturday to rehearse in the morning and then perform for our family and friends in the afternoon. My dad set up a canopy for our stage and brought out furniture for the set. When my friends arrived, we practiced and tried on costumes. Then we set up chairs for the audience. About 30 people showed up. We had a great time putting on the play. My favorite time was when one scene was supposed to take place during a rainstorm. My line was, "I wish it wasn't raining so I could go outside." To add realism to the play, my dad was in the back of the audience and sprayed everyone with a hose so they could experience rain!

Beacon Street Girls is another series of books created by Addie Swartz when she wanted more positive reading material for her daughters. The company's mission statement says:

Between Productions—home of the Beacon Street Girls—is dedicated to quality parent-approved literature, media and gifts for preteen girls who are between toys and boys. Shaped by experts in adolescent development and current research on how to positively impact girls' self-esteem, the award-winning Beacon Street Girls book series is committed to the health and well-being of tween girls. (www.beaconstreetgirls.com)

What could be wrong with that?

Magazines such as *Discovery Girls* and *Girls' Life* offer fun and wholesome reading material for your daughter. If she complains she'd rather read *Cosmopolitan*, remember that you're the mom!

> *Aleene, mother of two tweens:* "I was shocked to see what articles *Seventeen* was publishing! I let my daughters subscribe to *my* approved list of magazines. When an issue arrives, I offer to help them make a recipe or do a craft project from the magazine. That way we all look forward to using the magazine as a fun way to be together."

Susan, an administrative assistant and the mother of two tweens, shares a story about a time she took a stand against inappropriate media.

> "Once, my daughter had several friends over and I made the decision not to let them join friends to watch a certain movie. They ended up scrapbooking and having fun together. They went home with something they made. They had a good time without the movie."

Two of the hardest forms of media to control are the television and use of the computer. Actually, some parents tell me it's very easy. They simply set strict guidelines for "screen time."

> *Tammy, mother of a 13-year-old:* "Okay, I'm old fashioned. I just don't see why my kids need to watch TV for hours or sit in front of the

computer. We do two things: TV is off during the week, and each child can watch two hours on the weekend. The computer is in the living room where we can monitor the screen. If they need the computer for homework, fine. If not, find a book or something else to do. My daughter is still active in Girl Scouts and enjoys writing poetry and ice-skating. So far, she doesn't seem socially stunted from not watching *The OC*."

For most moms, Tammy's guidelines may be too restrictive. But then, my good friend Barb Brock has raised two creative, charming, delightful teenagers—without ever having a TV in their house! Consider some of the tips below for limiting screen time in your house. You're sure to find some ideas that fit your lifestyle. The point to remember is that *you* control the TV and computer. They shouldn't control your family!

Let's start with some sobering statistics from the TV-Turnoff Network:

- 40 percent of families always or often have the TV on during dinner.
- The TV is on a daily average of 7 hours, 40 minutes in the American home.
- 48 percent of children have a television in their bedroom.
- By the time a child is 18, he or she will have watched 200,000 acts of violence and 16,000 murders on TV.
- 91 percent of children say they feel "scared" or "worried" by violent scenes on TV.
- Parents spend an average of only 38.5 minutes a week in meaningful conversation with their children!

Check out their website, www.tvturnoff.org, for startling facts about the negative effects of TV on children.

Some families find it easiest to select two or three days a week when TV and computers are permitted. Your daughter will quickly learn she can have screen time on, say, Tuesdays, Thursdays, and Saturdays. On the other days, she has to find something else to do!

How about these ideas to limit TV time?

- Try putting the TV in a location that doesn't scream "Look at me! I'm this amazingly large TV that needs you to watch me for hours on end!" Delegate the TV to a family room or even the basement!
- One family had a built-in stipulation for watching TV: Whenever a commercial came on, you had to jog in place or do pushups or jumping jacks!
- Elaborate on television programs. For example, if your family enjoys "Shark Week" on the Discovery Channel, get some library books on sharks, visit an aquarium to see sharks close up, or make a papier-mâché shark as a table centerpiece. That way, TV is simply a supplement to educating and entertaining your family.

Sondra says: Our family loves Broadway musicals! I remember sitting on my dad's shoulders when I was three, with a curtain pullback draped over my shoulder.

We'd sing "Do You Hear the People Sing?" from the musical *Les Miserables*. I didn't understand the words, but I loved singing anyway.

We really like watching the Tony awards on TV—that's like the Oscars except the awards are theater related. One year, since we couldn't go to New York to actually see the Tonys, we brought New York to our family room. My dad and I took a long piece of butcher paper and drew the entire skyline of New York, with the Empire State Building and the Chrysler Building. We hung the 12-foot mural in the hall. Then we dug out the white Christmas lights and strung them everywhere to look like Times Square. They have the red carpet at the Tonys, so we taped red construction paper down the entire hall. Next, we prepared some fancy finger foods and poured sparkling cider in elegant plastic glasses. Then we all dressed up in our fanciest clothes, walked the red carpet, and sat among the lights of New York watching the Tony Awards—all in the comfort of our own home.

If all these ideas still seem too hard to cut back on TV time, then wait until the third week in April. It's National TV-Turnoff Week. Tell your family it's time to celebrate! This might be a great time to kick off the plan to limit your family's TV viewing.

If you're into technological devices, the TV Allowance may be what you need (check it out at www.tvallowance.com). This controller lets parents designate when and for how long the TV can be on. It even allows you to have custom settings for each child.

Consider designating certain chores to be equivalent to 30 minutes of TV viewing—complete the chore to Mom's satisfaction and you can watch some TV. Your daughter will learn that her actions can bring rewards. One mother gives her daughter five dollars above her regular allowance and then charges a dollar an hour to watch TV; no TV and she can use the extra money for something else. Other families find it works best to equate TV time with physical exercise. If your daughter plays soccer for 30 minutes, then she watches TV for the same amount of time.

We had a very unique experience when our family was asked to appear on the Fox reality show *Trading Spouses*. Yes, even though we hardly watch TV, we ended up appearing on TV! For this show, I spent a week living with a family in another state while their mom stayed with Allan and Sondra. Even though I didn't know the ages of the children, I packed an assortment of craft supplies such as fabric crayons, wooden race cars to decorate, cardboard dinosaurs, and a kaleidoscope-making kit. I also brought books and even a parachute for group games.

Upon arriving at the new home, I discovered that the three children, ages 8, 12, and 17, spent their summer days watching R-rated TV and videos for 14 to 16 hours a day. Breakfast consisted of coffee. Around noon, the kids complained about headaches. Dad kept telling me his 8-year-old daughter had ADHD, was hyperactive, and was a poor reader (in front of his daughter). Lunch consisted of ice cream eaten directly from the carton while watching more TV.

The show is designed that, for the first two days, I had to fit into their lifestyle, which meant sitting on the couch watching TV. (This was the hardest part of the entire experience!) But on the third day, I was able to declare, "Now we'll do things *my* way."

The first change was turning off the TV. Horrors! Instead of watching TV, we went hiking and rode bikes. I sent the shell-shocked dad off with his kids to go bowling and visit a museum. He was used to sitting in his leather recliner watching TV while working from home.

Then the crafts appeared. We started with the family making kaleidoscopes. The very macho dad made constant negative comments, including four-letter words that weren't "glue" and "lace." He called his 12-year-old son a "sissy" for enjoying the craft project. Throughout the next four days, the two younger kids kept asking if I had more crafts. We designated a shelf to display their creations for their mom. The TV crew bought more supplies because the family didn't even have colored markers or construction paper. The supposedly hyperactive 8-year-old spent two hours intensely mixing paint colors together. She'd never used paints and was fascinated that red and white paint created pink. I brought out the parachute when friends came over, and we played games together. No one complained of being bored.

On the day I left, the dad sheepishly said, "I actually had fun doing some of those crazy things you had us do." (Of course, he could have simply been saying that out of relief that I was leaving his house!) The kids flourished. They had time to read and draw detailed pictures. I spent an afternoon with the 8-year-old talking about the word *whimsical*. She dressed in whimsical clothes, and we designed quite the whimsical hairstyle, complete with a toilet roll and numerous multicolored ribbons. This family basically went cold turkey when it came to watching TV. It was a unique situation, yet it shows it's possible to get kids engaged in creative activities—even kids used to watching TV 14 to 16 hours a day! I'm sure they turned the TV on the minute I left the house, but both parents did tell me they were going to make a serious attempt to cut back on TV time.

As Groucho Marx said, "I find television very educating. Every time somebody turns on the set, I go into the other room and read a book."

Just for Fun

Believe me, this *can* be fun! Quietly monitor the amount of TV your family watches in one week. Then set a week aside when you'll simply cut that amount in half. Make an announcement like, "Hello, Taylor family! Last week, I recorded that the TV was on for 25 hours. Beginning July 16, we're going to cut that amount in half. Therefore, from July 16–22, we'll watch $12\frac{1}{2}$ hours. However, to take the place of TV, here are some things we can do." Then show a few games you've purchased, a gift certificate at an ice cream parlor, and just a few ideas for family walks and activities.

How about making homemade root beer? Just follow these super-easy directions: Bring $1\frac{1}{2}$ cups water to a boil. Add $\frac{3}{4}$ cup sugar and stir. Add $1\frac{1}{2}$ teaspoons root beer concentrate (available in any grocery store). Put the mixture in the refrigerator to cool. When ready to enjoy your treat, pour 1 liter of cold soda water or club soda into the root beer mixture. Add ice cream, and you have homemade root beer floats!

As you cut back on TV time, you'll probably get a few groans from family members. In this case, overlook the groans, put on your best activity-director persona, and show your family that life exists beyond the world of TV. Besides, it's just for one week!

Chapter 7

It's Not Always about You

The last time your daughter had friends over, I'm sure you probably heard this conversation:

> "I think we should all collect hats and gloves and donate them to poor people."
>
> "Does anyone want to help me tomorrow? I'm going to surprise my Grandma and help clean her house."
>
> "My little sister isn't feeling well. I'll be right back. I'm going to go read her a story."
>
> "My cell phone is getting old, but it still works, so I'll keep it."
>
> "Let's ask that new girl to sit with us at lunch tomorrow. It must be scary walking into the cafeteria and not knowing anyone."

Okay, you would need to be in the Twilight Zone to hear comments like that. More than likely, you heard snippets of conversation such as:

> "I *have* to get my mom to buy me those jeans! I'll be a dork if I don't look like everyone else."
>
> "But I want a *new* cell phone! This one is six months old."
>
> "I want my birthday party at the spa. That way I'll be known as the girl with the really cool party."
>
> "Okay, okay, I know there are poor people in the world, but I don't want to go serve soup at the smelly homeless shelter."

While it would be wonderful if your tween thought about others and exhibited totally selfless behavior, she's probably thinking only about herself. Unfortunately, self-absorbed girls grow up to be self-absorbed adults.

Actually, it makes sense that our daughters feel the world revolves around them. They burst from our wombs hearing how smart, funny, clever, bright, gifted, quick, beautiful, charming, creative, delightful, and all-around amazing they were. Then when our talented tween daughters display selfish behavior, we wonder why they can't think of others occasionally.

> *Betty, a mom with two tween daughters:* "I get so upset at my daughters' selfish habits. All they think about is themselves. I had to fight with my 12-year-old to get her to send a birthday card to her grandmother. My daughters want new clothes, fancy computers, and highlighted hair. I just want them to see how self-centered they are."

> *Mandy, a church secretary and the mother of an 11-year-old, about her daughter:* "Selfish, selfish, selfish. That is what causes fights. 'I want.' 'Me.' 'Mine.' Sometimes the focus is Maddie. Sometimes the focus is me. My princess learned her sense of entitlement from me!"

Yes, sometimes as moms we have to make a conscious effort to teach our daughters that they are not the center of the universe.

> *Mary, an executive in Nashville with an 11-year-old daughter:* "We are in transition, and I realize I've been too busy—working at my company, traveling, building a house and an office building for the last 11 years—to teach my daughter the importance of cleaning up after herself. We had cleaning help, and she didn't clean when told, so the cleaning people did it. Now that we've moved, it is a mess! I am trying to get her to be responsible for herself and help more for the common good. I let it slip before because I felt that I was so busy that the family needed to have fun during free time and to have the 'snuggle time' that my daughter needed so much."

There's good news when it comes to helping children learn caring, responsibility, and empathy. Researchers show that altruistic behavior is actually a learned trait. So here's another task for your to-do list: Teach your daughter to be altruistic.

Just exactly what is altruism? Basically, it's the ability to put the welfare of others above yourself. (In the case of tweens, this also includes putting the welfare of animals before your own.) Researchers at Duke Medical Center in North Carolina found a part of the brain that behaves differently between altruistic and selfish people. Through a series of tests and brain scans, the scientists discovered that altruistic people were able to tune into the actions and facial features of others. Altruistic people perceive other people's actions as important. In other words, selfless people see the value in other people. (If you really like scientific information, read the entire article in the ever-popular *Nature Neuroscience*, February 2007 edition.)

How can you help your daughter understand that other people also have needs, wants, failures, and successes? Try some of these activities to give your daughter the knowledge that "it's not always about her."

- Once again, it's up to us to model positive behavior. Hold the door open for someone entering the bank. Look the grocery store cashier in the eyes as you pay your bill. One family had a routine of always picking up their shopping cart from the parking lot and taking it into the store. This was one less cumbersome cart a clerk had to bring back inside. Model polite behavior when your own mother makes a sarcastic comment about your housekeeping capabilities. (At least try!)

- Explain why you treat people a certain way. Let your daughter know her little brother's painful ear infection puts him in a cranky mood. Tell her, "We'll have to be extra patient with Peter because his ear really hurts." If your daughter is busy with the last few days of dress rehearsal for the sixth-grade play, explain that you'll make her bed the next three days because of her schedule.

- Help her imagine how other people feel. Set up miniscenarios such as: "Let's pretend I came home from work with lots of phone calls to make. I hadn't gone grocery shopping, and Grandpa was coming over for dinner. I'd asked you to straighten up the living room, but you were watching TV. How do you think I'd feel?" When your daughter complains about a teacher keeping the class inside for recess, encourage her to put herself in her teacher's place. What would she do to get a class of rowdy students to do their work? If you walk by a mother with a screaming toddler, ask your daughter why she thinks the baby is upset. Is the baby's behavior affecting his mother? How do moms feel when their precious darling throws a fit in public? (This is a great time to share with your daughter about a time she had a tantrum in public!)

- Check out the Girl Scout programs in your area. The "Studio 2B2" is designed specifically for teens (see www.studio2B2.org). Your daughter will have the opportunity to participate in programs dealing with careers, peer pressure, hobbies, and community service. She'll learn from practical experience that it's not always about her. Of course, other worthwhile Girl Scout programs also exist for younger girls.

- Point out rude and kind behavior on TV. How did the 10-year-old treat her sister on that cereal commercial? Was it polite for that dad to give a snide reply to the clerk in the car rental commercial? Would your daughter be willing to save your life by giving up her kidney like on the Hallmark Hall of Fame special? (Okay, that's too dramatic!) Watch a rerun of *The Cosby Show*. The family's love and caring for each other is evident in each episode. Compare the Cosby family with Bart Simpson's sarcastic behavior.

- Point out other people's facial expressions (unobtrusively, of course!). Ask your daughter, "What was the clerk's face like when I asked to see a picture of her baby?" Have your daughter glance at the people in the car next to you while waiting at a stoplight. Are they fighting? Do they look in a hurry to get home? You'll be surprised how often your daughter isn't even aware that other people around her have problems and feelings just like her!

- If possible, try a "Freaky Friday" and switch places with your daughter. This doesn't mean you need to wear a miniskirt and trot off to middle school. Try switching places on a Saturday morning. You watch cartoons while your daughter cleans up the breakfast dishes, does three loads of laundry, sweeps the kitchen floor, vacuums the car, and walks the dog. Sometimes just an hour of your life will give your daughter an eye-opening experience of putting herself in your place.

- Give your daughter real-life experiences when it comes to budgeting, meeting deadlines, and having responsibility. If she doesn't take the puppy outside, make her clean up its mess on the carpet.

> *Theresa, a disaster recovery administrator:* "My daughter Hailey will be 12 in May. I have been divorced for the past two and a half years, and I would have to say the best thing I have done to keep our relationship positive is to let her 'in' on the finances. She and I discuss money very openly with respect to how there is just one pot of money and how do we want to spend it—how not going into debt gives us peace of mind and that saving our money for the future is a necessity. This has helped us so much with regard to the pressures kids get regarding cell phones, computer games, clothes, designer tennis shoes. The conversations are so much easier because she understands how money works. She also has a newfound wisdom with respect to the money she earns and how she wants to spend it."

Mother-Daughter Mini-Activity

Get a coffee table–type book of Norman Rockwell paintings and look at them with your daughter. His dramatic yet real-life paintings of everyday situations are a great starting place to talk about each character and what they are feeling in that particular picture. My favorite is his drawing of a smiling pigtailed girl with a black eye and scuffed knees sitting in front of the principal's office. Have your daughter tell you why she thinks the girl got in a fight, and why the girl looks so pleased with herself.

One of the best ways to help your daughter learn that the world doesn't revolve around her is to get her to reach outside herself and do volunteer work. Before you have visions of your petite 9-year-old serving soup to unshaven homeless men at a rescue mission, relax. Countless volunteer opportunities exist that are safe and fun, yet still teach valuable lessons. Here's another reason to get your daughter volunteering: According to a study by the Search Institute, youths who volunteer just one hour a week are 50 percent less likely to abuse drugs, alcohol, and cigarettes or to engage in destructive behavior.

As your daughter begins volunteering, she'll do more than help people, animals, or the environment. She'll gain valuable life-lessons. Here are four skills your daughter develops while volunteering:

1. Volunteering teaches responsibility. Did your daughter sign up to help plant flowers at the senior center? She'll learn that it's important she shows up on time and does her part to help. Yes, her hands get dirty and she's hot working in the sun. But the group relies on volunteers to brighten the flower gardens for seniors. Is your daughter responsible to make posters advertising an upcoming book drive? Once again, she'll see that her efforts are needed to make the drive a success. If the signs aren't made, people won't know about the sale.

2. Volunteering teaches empathy for people and animals. Yes, it's hard walking through an animal shelter and seeing sad-eyed dogs gazing at you from behind their chain-link cages. But if your daughter never sees dogs in a shelter, she'll never know the importance of telling people to get identification tags for their pets. Older tweens begin to understand the importance of spaying or neutering pets to avoid unwanted puppies and kittens. As your daughter empathizes with homeless pets, she will learn that her effort at walking dogs or collecting used tennis balls helps pets have a better life. See if there's a local Special Olympics team in your community. Spend time with your daughter volunteering with some very enthusiastic athletes! Even a 9-year-old can work with a Special Olympics athlete, teaching him or her to stay in their designated lane during a track event, for example.

3. Volunteering teaches kids about their community. Most tweens think their world involves only school, the mall, soccer fields, and in some cases, church. By exposing your daughter to volunteer organizations, she gains broader exposure to her community. When donating books to a Head Start preschool, she will see that some schools aren't as well equipped as hers. If you take your daughter to a program that teaches disabled children to ride horses, she'll learn about various types of therapy. Does the senior citizen center need help sorting canned goods? Take your daughter, so she'll see resources available to the elderly.

4. Volunteering helps children develop relationships with caring adults. As your daughter works side by side with adults on volunteer projects, she will meet adults who are positive role models. She'll talk to people who will willingly share why they volunteer. Your daughter will be surrounded by people who eagerly get up at 6:00 AM to participate in a bald eagle count or who spend hours crocheting hats for at-risk babies. Instead of looking up to rock stars advocating skimpy clothes and premarital sex, your daughter might just tell you, "Mom! Mrs. Jefferson is so cool! Do you know she trains puppies that will become Seeing Eye dogs to help the blind? She said I can help her!"

When it comes to giving more ideas on volunteering, I think I'll let Sondra take over. She's had amazing experiences of travel, meeting people, and helping others, simply through her volunteer efforts.

Sondra says: When I was 11, I read a book about Jane Goodall and decided to turn my room into a Jane Goodall research station. We put up huge bamboo poles, which we decorated with vines and stuffed monkeys. My Mom and I sponge-painted leaves on the wall so I felt I was in the jungle. My dad and I even made a wooden sign to hang above my door that said "Sondra Clark Research Station." That's been a few years, but I'm still influenced by something she wrote in her book. She said: "Do the small things. Pick up the phone or write a letter. And never let anyone tell you it doesn't make a difference." That phrase stuck with me as I began doing volunteer work for AIDS orphans in Africa.

When you and your daughter hear the word *volunteering*, what's the first image that comes to your mind? Donating your outgrown clothes to the Salvation Army? Maybe you think volunteering means you have to go to Africa and live in a mud hut and eat raw bugs while teaching Sunday School to starving children. Actually, those *are* ways to volunteer, yet the world of volunteering is much broader than the stereotypical ideas most people have.

There are hundreds of ways to volunteer, from collecting newspapers for the Humane Society to playing the guitar at an assisted living center. There's a volunteer possibility just right for your daughter. I have a friend who loves gymnastics, so she volunteers at a local gym and teaches kids to somersault and do cartwheels. That's a long way from eating raw bugs in Africa! She found something that she loved doing and gives her time helping others.

Because I enjoy public speaking, I've volunteered by speaking at churches, service clubs, and schools, telling people how they can help kids in developing countries. Sometimes it's a bit scary to get up in front of a couple thousand people, but the results are worth it. I've learned it's not about me. I may be tired or scared to speak to a group, but that doesn't matter. What matters is that I think about how my actions are helping other people.

Those speaking engagements have given me the opportunity to travel around the country and meet lots of wonderful people. Okay, every once in a while I also get to be on a TV show to talk about volunteering. Getting picked up in a limo is not a bad way to volunteer!

You may not want your daughter packing her bags and heading off to Africa, but she can learn to think about others while volunteering. Here are some other benefits:

- She'll learn new skills while volunteering.
- Volunteering lets you make a positive difference in the world.
- She'll learn there's more to life than worrying about that pimple on her nose or the fight with her best friend.
- It's a great chance for her to meet people with similar interests.
- She might get school credit for volunteering.

When I was 11 years old, I was given the opportunity to travel to Kenya and Uganda. We visited one island where more than 50 percent of the population had AIDS. It was tragic to see children become orphans because their parents were dying. I met a 10-year-old boy named Eric, whose father had died and mother was slowly dying of AIDS. His mother knew she couldn't care for him, so she applied at a relief agency to have Eric live in a group home. My parents and I were with their staff when they went to pick up Eric and take him to the group home. It was heartbreaking to see his mother say goodbye to him. We knew it was probably the last time they would see each other. Eric walked with us down a jungle path to our car. He brought nothing with him, because he didn't even own an extra set of clothes. Later, a school principal asked if I wanted to see the school library. Naturally I said yes, and he proudly led me to the library. It was simply a small bookcase with about 35 tattered books. Most of your daughters have more books than that in their bedroom.

When I got back from Africa, I knew I needed to do something, so I organized a book drive. With my Girl Scout troop, we collected three hundred books to send to Africa along with boxes of school supplies like posters, markers, and worksheets. Last summer I decided I wanted to give the kids I met some fun in their lives, so I started a project called Fun with a Future. I collected a thousand Frisbee-type discs for kids to play with. I then collected 5,000 toothbrushes and 10,000 pens and pencils to help the kids with their future.

When I speak to different groups, kids always come up and ask me how they can get involved in volunteering. The first thing I do is ask about their interests. If your daughter is shy, she certainly won't want to sing at a senior center. Here are some ideas I suggest to kids. Read them together with your daughter and see if any ideas interest her.

If you like working with animals:

- Local shelters need people to help walk the dogs and to play with the cats. Because the animals don't have homes yet, they have no one to love and care for them. Call the local shelter and see if they need people to play with the animals. If they say yes, get a group of friends together and make it a fun afternoon!

- If you have an elderly neighbor with a dog, see if they need help walking their dog. Many times, seniors don't have the energy to give their dogs the exercise they need. Offer to take the dog for walks—with adult permission, of course!

- Volunteering doesn't always have to mean going out and doing something. You can volunteer and make a difference by buying only products that aren't tested on animals. PETA has great lists that catalog all the companies that don't test on animals.

- Collect pet food from friends and neighbors and donate it to senior citizen pet food banks. Seniors get very attached to their pets but often are on a limited income. Government-issued food stamps don't allow seniors to buy pet food, so your donation really helps.

Volunteering from home:

- Look through your closet; I'm sure you have shirts you've outgrown or pants that are so last season. Why not put those to use? Donate your slightly used clothing to a women's shelter or a local clothing drive. Does an older sister have a prom dress she'll never wear again? Several national organizations collect prom dresses to give to girls that can't afford to buy their own. Check out www.beccascloset.com for a place to donate the dresses.

- Ask your family to help you sponsor a child in a developing country. A great organization that only spends 4 percent of its budget on administration is

Childcare Worldwide (www.childcareworldwide.org). For $35 a month, you can help a child get food, medicine, spiritual training, and a chance to go to school and break the cycle of poverty. I actually got to meet the girl I sponsor in Africa, which was an amazing experience! I saw how my money has changed her life.

See? Didn't I tell you there were many ways to help your daughter volunteer? If you want even more ideas, check out my book *You Can Change Your World!* It gives more than a hundred additional ways to get involved in volunteer projects. As you consider volunteer possibilities, remember that what you do doesn't have to be grandiose. As Jane Goodall said, "Do the small things. Pick up the phone or write a letter. And never let anyone tell you it doesn't make a difference."

One mother asked me, "How can I volunteer when I have various-aged kids? I know it's important to volunteer, but we don't have time."

The wonderful thing about volunteering is that it can be a family activity or a mother-daughter project. Adults gain from the experience as much as children. A great resource is *The Busy Family's Guide to Volunteering: Doing Good Together* by Jenny Friedman. The book gives practical ideas on how to incorporate volunteer projects into your busy life. Sondra just signed a contract to write a book called *77 Awesome Volunteer Activities*. The easy-to-follow format will give step-by-step directions on how kids can take part in creative volunteer activities. Look for it in early 2008!

Can't volunteer on a regular basis? How about trying to do one volunteer project a month? Follow this simple schedule to get in the habit of volunteering.

January: Make a New Year's resolution to volunteer in some program or activity at least once a month with your daughter. (See how easy that was?)

February: Celebrate Girls and Women in Sports Day on or around February 4. Contact your local Special Olympics program and offer to coach a female athlete. Have your daughter write a thank-you card to a female coach in her life. www.womenssportsfoundation.org. This site gives scholarship and grant information for girls' sports programs. Your daughter can also look at the "Inspiration Station" and read inspirational stories about female athletes.

March: Help celebrate National Kids Craft Day on March 14. Go with your daughter and volunteer to teach a craft project to an after-school program or scout troop. Get great craft supplies from S&S Worldwide (www.ssww.com).

April: Join millions of other youth in volunteering on National Youth Service Day in mid-April (see www.ysa.org/nysd).

May: Get moving during National Fitness and Sports Month. With your daughter, volunteer to lead a walk around your neighborhood on a Saturday when most kids stay inside watching cartoons.

June: June is designated as Great Outdoors Month. Contact your local parks and recreation department or state park to check out special programs they offer. The www.gorving.com website has fun outdoor activities under "Hit the Road." You'll get ideas for outdoor games, great road trips, and outdoor cooking recipes. They'll even send you a free DVD or CD-ROM with more information on RV camping.

July: Celebrate National Literacy Day this entire month. Volunteer at the library story hour by reading a book and having your daughter dress as one of the characters. Ask your neighbors for book donations and donate them to a children's hospital or a Ronald McDonald house.

August: It's Be an Angel Day on August 22. Find a way for you and your daughter to be kind and helpful to someone. How about writing Grandma an actual letter or secretly putting flowers on a neighbor's doorstep?

September: This is National School Success Month. Ask your friends to buy an extra notebook or pack of pencils when they buy school supplies. Donate those items to a school for disadvantaged children.

October: Use this month to get ready for National Make a Difference Day on the fourth Saturday of the month. Plan a community cleanup program, collect used towels for the local animal shelter, or help paint a senior's house. For more ideas, go to www.usatoday.com/diffday.

November: Get your family involved by celebrating National Family Volunteer Day on the third Saturday of November (see www.pointsoflight.org/organiztions/nfvd.cfm).

December: Work with your daughter and friends to plan an afternoon of safe, fun activities for kids. Parents can drop off their children and go holiday shopping. Ask for donations, which you give to the charity of your choice.

Just think what a difference it will make in your daughter's way of thinking if she volunteers once a month. She'll suddenly be aware of how she *can* make a difference, even as a tween. Her world will expand beyond the latest Lindsay Lohan escapade to understanding what it takes to put on an art show or collect cans of food for a pet food bank. Try to be creative and find volunteer projects that work into your family's lifestyle.

One family with three children found a unique way to volunteer. After their Sunday morning church service, the family went to the church nursery. Their volunteer project? Disinfecting baby toys! They washed all the plastic toys with a mild soap and bleach solution and wiped down the countertops and changing tables. The process took only 15 minutes but served a real purpose and gave the family a volunteer activity to do together. Another mom found a great way to communicate with her own daughter while helping a neighbor with a new baby. On Mondays, Wednesdays, and Fridays, she and her daughter took the neighbor's baby for a walk in the stroller. You can imagine how grateful the harried young mother was for a break, while Mom and tween daughter had fun "babysitting."

Sondra says: Your daughter might not be excited about volunteering. To put things in perspective, suggest the following ideas. Then she will probably be more than happy to paint birdhouses for a nursing home than doing any of the activities on this list!

- Tooth brusher at a crocodile ranch
- Underarm hair counter
- Judge for a "smelliest sneaker" contest
- Bad-breath evaluator
- Elephant "droppings" inspector
- Dirty toilet unplugger
- St. Bernard slobber collector
- Pig cleaner after a greased pig contest
- Confetti collector after the New Year's party in Times Square

The point of Sondra's list is to have a lighthearted attitude toward volunteering. Giving your daughter a lecture of, "You have such a good life. You need to know how lucky you are, so we're going to go down to a halfway house for alcoholics and you have to clean 15 toilets!" isn't the best approach. Start with a few nonthreatening volunteer projects, like baking cookies and secretly leaving them at your daughter's dance teacher's house. As your daughter gets comfortable volunteering, you can handle more "serious" projects.

For example, after Hurricane Katrina hit the Gulf Coast, our family decided to offer our services as volunteers. Because Sondra knew that volunteering sometimes requires sacrifice, we actually left on Christmas Day to drive to the Biloxi area. It wasn't a traditional way to spend the holidays. Instead of casually opening presents while drinking hot chocolate, we put on face masks and ripped down moldy drywall from storm-ravaged houses. We sorted mountains of donated clothing and distributed it to people needing basic supplies, all the while sleeping on the floor of a church preschool. Would we do it again? Of course! Our family could open presents any day. Instead, we saw a need and decided to help. Experiences such as helping survivors of Katrina gave us all an appreciation for what we have. As we met other volunteer families, we also learned the power of many people working together.

In looking over our surveys submitted by tween girls, many girls commented on feeling unimportant, not valued. Lonnie, an 11-year-old, wrote:

> "Sometimes I feel like I'm too young to do anything! My mom won't let me go to the mall with friends. I can't ride my bike to a friend's house. You have to be 12 to join the dance program I want to do. I can't get a job, so I don't have any money."

Lonnie is right. It's hard for 11-year-olds to feel old enough to do anything "significant." That's where volunteering comes in.

Volunteering is a way for girls to be connected with a "higher purpose." Instead of worrying about what color their new backpack should be, girls involved in volunteering know that some kids don't even own a backpack. They develop empathy for students unable to afford fancy vacations and designer clothes. The researchers at Duke University Medical Center said altruism can be learned. Your daughter will learn that it's not all about her as she sees you modeling caring behavior. By putting herself in the other person's place, she'll begin to look beyond her petty perspective. Add to that a few volunteer experiences and you have a kind daughter on the way to thinking and respecting other people.

> *Eleanor, mother of a 13-year-old:* "The best part of having a tween daughter is seeing her blossom into a confident, caring young woman. She's getting 'flashes' of time when she thinks about a situation from another person's point of view. She's taking action when someone picks on the 'underdog' at school. I think there's hope for this generation!"

Need more ideas on helping your daughter look beyond herself? Look at www.parentingteens.org. This website, run by the child care professionals at Girls and Boys Town, gives ideas for effective communication skills as well as developmental guidelines.

Just for Fun

Set aside a time when you and your daughter can make some Bedtime Snack Sacks. Your daughter probably enjoys an occasional bedtime snack. (Don't we all like a few cookies and milk before we go to bed?) Explain how children living in women's shelters don't have the chance to get bedtime snacks. Set out an assortment of markers, stickers, sequins, and ribbons, and decorate ordinary lunch bags with your craft supplies. Then fill each bag with a juice pack, a nonperishable snack like granola bars or raisins, and a "treat." Have your daughter find some Happy Meal–type toys or other small items in good condition to add to the sacks. That way, children in a shelter get a snack plus a new toy. Call a shelter and ask about the best time to deliver the Snack Sacks. Take your daughter along so she understands what a homeless shelter looks like. You probably won't be able to meet the children for security reasons, but an administrator will thank you and your daughter.

Chapter 8

Give Her a Go Get 'em Attitude

A few weeks ago, I saw a bumper sticker on the back of a fancy water-ski boat that read: "He who dies with the most toys, wins." I didn't agree with that sage advice and gave it little extra thought. A few days later, I saw a similar bumper sticker on the back of a well-traveled van that made more sense. This one read: "He who dies with the most experiences, wins."

As Sondra and I distributed surveys to moms across the country, one comment kept appearing over and over, such as this one from a mom and administrative assistant: "All my daughter wants to do is either hang out at the mall or play games on the computer. How can I show her there's more to life than picking out earrings at Claire's?"

As mothers of tween daughters, we have the ability to expose our daughters to a world beyond the typical routine of watching TV, shopping, and playing video games. It takes effort, but the result is a daughter with the ability to look beyond herself and have a global perspective. Plus, you'll both have some great experiences!

When Allan and I were dating, we found ourselves in the typical rut of going out for pizza and a movie. (Videos and DVDs didn't even exist back then!) He came up with the idea of "Educational Experiences." Each week, one of us had the responsibility to come up with an all-new, inexpensive activity for a date. The event would be kept secret, so we never knew what the other one was planning. We began enjoying some amazing experiences!

On one occasion, Allan took me to see a slide show by a world-famous anthropologist. She showed pictures of skulls that had evidently caused quit a stir in the "skull community." As she showed each slide (which all looked identical to Allan and me), the audience would gasp or whisper, "Unbelievable!" "What an amazing specimen!" Sometimes they broke out in applause because a particular skull had a highly defined arch in the nose. Who would have thought groups of people could enjoy looking at nose arches on skulls on a Saturday night?

Another time, we visited a Mexican hairless dog show. In my opinion, these have to be the ugliest dogs in existence! Yet their owners groomed and kissed their hairless wonders as if they were as cute as my springer spaniel. We had breakfast at a grange, played bingo at a senior center, and dug through garbage to help with a recycling project. One time we attended opening night at a theater and were the only ones in the audience!

Allan and I enjoyed our Educational Experiences so much that we've continued them through 29 years of marriage (not every week though!). Both Trina and Sondra have grown up hearing, "We have an Educational Experience at 9:00 AM on Saturday. Dress warm." The only rule is that no one is allowed to complain about the event. We're taking a risk by going to an "unknown" event, so no one can be negative.

Last week, I read about an event that I thought would be a great Educational Experience. Suzan-Lori Parks, a Pulitzer Prize–winning playwright, has written six hundred plays. Sounds impressive, doesn't it? That's what I thought, until I found out her plays last just two to five minutes each! Vanderbilt University announced the opportunity to see 10 of her plays in its theater. "Educational Experience at noon on Saturday," I announced to my family.

On the appointed day, we arrived to join 25 or so people shivering in the wind outside the theater. Snow was expected that afternoon, and the temperature seemed to drop every second. Suddenly a student announced, "All the plays will be performed outside!" Within 20 seconds, the performance started. At least, we *think* it started, because some students yelled and threw themselves on the frozen ground. Another student held a sword over her head and collapsed. End of the first play. The theatrical extravaganza continued with a series of microplays taken from the theater of the absurd. The plays had no beginning, middle, or end. Unless an actor really projected, the wind would carry their voice across campus—away from the audience. The sun disappeared, the wind cut through our coats, and the three of us laughed because once again we were taking part in an Educational Experience. Thank goodness all 10 plays lasted for a total of only 34 minutes!

When I look at Sondra's capability to adjust to new situations, I know part of that comes from her Educational Experiences. Ever since she was little, there were so many events that got all of us out of our comfort zone. When you're taking a behind-the-scenes tour of a bakery or helping judge a kid's dog show, you gain valuable coping skills. On one occasion we attended an inner-city church service on Martin Luther King Jr. Day. Suddenly the three of us looked around and saw we were the only Caucasians in the church! That experience produced many conversations about what it feels like to be a minority.

Sondra says: Although I might complain about my parents and their crazy ideas, I love them. I have been put into so many strange situations that I really don't have a comfort zone any more.

I was attending a journalism conference, and the teacher used me as an example to make his point. He was attempting to show the class that, as a journalist, there are some subjects you just can't fake your way through. He asked if I would be willing to give a minispeech on obscure topics. Of course, I said yes. The first topic he presented was "Peruvian Art in the 18th Century." Having recently returned from Peru, where we visited several art museums, I obviously started talking about the subject with confidence and real facts. He was a bit taken back, so he gave me another topic. He asked me to discuss some aspect of gay culture. I launched into a description of how my parents had taken me to a gay pride parade in San Francisco and the parade participants threw condoms into the crowd. The professor took another stab at having me talk about a difficult subject. "OK" he said. "Since this is a writer's conference, discuss the business aspects of writing and publishing a book." I was on a roll! Having written seven books, it was easy to discuss all the aspects of book publishing, from getting an agent to writing a proposal, negotiating a contract, selling foreign rights, and so on! The professor and I had a good laugh about his exercise. I'm not super-smart. I've just had lots of experiences that give me the ability to start a conversation with anyone about anything. I have been put in unusual situations that certainly give me a go get 'em attitude!

You don't have to take your daughter to Peru or have her write books. She can get similar experiences by attending free cultural events or meeting authors at free book-signing events.

Mother-Daughter Mini-Activity

Take your daughter on an Educational Experience. Simply listen to the radio when they announce community events, or look in the newspaper. Most papers have weekend guides listing all the clubs, festivals, and special events taking place during the week. You and your daughter will get to experience a new situation—together. It may be amazingly interesting or amazingly boring! Either way, you'll create a lasting memory of an "unknown" activity involving you and your daughter.

I just opened our local paper, *The Tennessean*, and found these two activities ideal for an Educational Experience. (Not that you have to come to Nashville, but I want to make the point that opportunities are everywhere.

1. A local college is providing an "Explore Your Brain" day and will have actual human brains available for people to hold. Rubber gloves provided!

2. The mayor of Nashville is leading a hike through a park, pointing out historical cemeteries.

So which would you prefer to do with your daughter? Stay home and watch cartoons, or hold a brain and visit a cemetery?

When Sondra was in sixth grade, I woke her up early to take her downtown to watch college students protesting the demolition of a historic building. It was a peaceful demonstration, as the students calmly erected metal poles in the ground, then chained themselves to the poles. The police, instead of forcing the protestors to leave, simply decided to wait out the situation. One police officer even shared his doughnut with a college student attached to the pole. Sondra and I sat across the street from the protestors, eating bagels and discussing what causes people to feel so strongly about an issue that they are willing to stay outside overnight, chained to a pole. You don't get that experience watching TV!

Think back to when your daughter was in preschool. She probably had the attitude of "Golly gee! The world is a great place!" Each day brought new opportunities to get ice cream with Grandma or pick out dress-up clothes at a garage sale. Your tween daughter has the capability to continue with her go get 'em attitude. It simply takes some effort on your part to give her new, positive experiences. (Even if the experience involves watching bizarre plays in cold weather.)

I recently met a woman at a social event. We did the usual chitchat, and then the conversation turned to travel. "I haven't ever traveled out of Tennessee," she said. "Someday I'd like to see the ocean." I immediately gave her my best tour guide speech, extolling the wonders of travel. I even mentioned a very low-cost flight from her hometown to Miami. She quickly told me she'd never fly due to the dangers of mechanical breakdown, terrorists, bad air, incompetent pilots, crying babies, and stale peanuts. "Okay," I countered. "Next chance you and your husband have, *drive* to the ocean. It's an amazing experience to feel the waves hit your legs." She looked at me in complete shock. "Oh, I'd never go in the water. I'd just look at the ocean from a distance." Do we want our daughters to live a life where they feel scared to feel ocean waves?

Lynn Ponton, a psychiatrist at the University of California, San Francisco, wrote a book called *The Romance of Risk* in which she encourages parents to help teens take healthy risks. She suggests parents get their teenagers to try out for the school play, run for office, or start a new hobby. When kids involve themselves in "safe" risks, they're less likely to pursue dangerous ones. As mothers, it's our job to steer our daughters away from risks such as self-mutilation and body piercing.

I encouraged Trina to take a healthy risk when she was 13. Our family got a great price on a ski trip to Zell am See, Austria. One afternoon, because the wind chill was −17 degrees on the mountain, we decided to play tourist and shop, instead of freezing on the ski slopes. A festival of sorts was going on, which meant hordes of people crowded the tiny Alpine streets. Trina and I agreed to meet Allan at a particular corner in 20 minutes. As we exited a store, we saw a hometown parade going by, with school kids and local dignitaries riding in the back of wagons. Oompah bands played, while spectators cheered their friends riding on the homemade floats. As a large trailer-type float approached, filled with people robustly singing in German and holding giant beer steins, I asked Trina, "Do you want to jump on that float and wave to Dad as he waits for us right down the street?" That's a risk, isn't it? But it seemed like an appropriate one. What could they do besides kick us off the float? We quickly hopped on the trailer, acting as if we were scheduled to be part of the group, and began waving to the crowd. Trina and I have a fond memory of seeing Allan's startled face as we waved from the float in our impromptu parade participation.

Think back to the last time you took a healthy risk. Did you decide to change jobs? Maybe you joined a book club with a group of strangers. I recently got up the nerve to join the YMCA. Even though I travel around the world (often by myself) encouraging people to take risks, I was scared to walk into the fitness area. Those machines looked too complicated. At what speed do I set the treadmill? How do I lift the weights? And most important, where do I plug in my headset? I had butterflies in my stomach walking in for the first time. Put me in front of five hundred people and I can give a great speech, but this was totally out of my comfort zone. Nevertheless, after getting some help from a staff member, I was soon sweating away with the rest of the slightly plump middle-aged women. As I left, a feeling of accomplishment replaced the previous butterflies. All evening, I told my family, "I worked out at the Y! I worked out at the Y!" That act boosted my feeling of self-confidence. Today the Y! Tomorrow I start training for a marathon! (I'll have to think that one over.)

Children also benefit from healthy risk taking. Samantha, a 12-year-old, wrote on her survey, "Sometimes I get so bored. All I do after school is watch TV and fight with my brother. I wish I had something to do."

According to the U.S. Fire Administration, 53 percent of fires are started by children under the age of 18. With children ages 10–14, the two main reasons for starting fires are boredom and peer pressure. One 10-year-old who repeatedly set fires told authorities that he liked watching the results of his risky behavior. His actions produced speeding trucks, loud sirens, and real-life action heroes. The excitement relieved his boredom.

If your daughter is getting a positive "adrenaline rush" from participating in a kid's talent show at the community center or learning to ride a horse, she's more likely to avoid unhealthy risks such as starting fires.

> *Janice, mother of a 9-year-old:* "I hear so many horror stories about girls going wild when they reach middle school. What can I do to keep my daughter from taking drugs or hanging out with the wrong crowd?"

There's no guarantee your daughter will turn into a perfect, straight-A, witty, creative, kind, generous Rhodes Scholar that loves her mother. But most experts agree that girls with positive self-images have a strong chance of "staying out of trouble." The following are some suggestions to help steer your daughter toward activities where she can learn about appropriate risk taking, which in turn will boost her self-esteem—which produces a go get 'em attitude.

- Encourage physical activities (under supervision, of course) beyond the usual soccer and gymnastics programs. How about rock climbing, ice-skating, karate, kickboxing, white-water rafting, horseback riding, or Frisbee golf? Take her "glow-in-the-light" bowling, where everything is lit with fluorescent colors and black-light machines make her white T-shirt totally bright-white.
- Have your daughter try creative activities such as writing poetry, practicing photography, starting a band, trying out for a community play, making a video, or teaching some friends dance routines.
- Put your daughter in new situations where she'll meet a variety of people. Can she read to children at a preschool? How about helping make Valentine's Day table decorations at a senior center? Find a volunteer project that the entire family can get involved with. See if a neighbor wants to hire your daughter as a mother's helper after school.
- Travel as often as possible with your daughter. These don't need to be shopping sprees to Paris. A simple trip to an arts festival in a nearby community will give you both risk-taking experience. How will you find the festival? Teach your daughter to read a map or use MapQuest. As you travel, look for regional differences. Moving to Nashville from Seattle has introduced us to sweet tea. If you're at the airport, let your daughter take the lead in finding your gate, going through security, and even filling out a claim for lost baggage!

Of course, you don't have to have your daughter do every one of these activities. She just needs occasional new risk-taking experiences to help her develop that go get 'em attitude. With each new experience, she'll gain confidence in meeting new challenges. Once she has successfully played the piano at the senior center, she'll feel more comfortable playing at a large school assembly.

At a meeting for parents of sixth-graders, the principal told us, "Don't be surprised if your son or daughter needs four months to adjust to middle school and changing rooms for each class. More than half the students need that amount of time to feel comfortable moving from room to room and coping with multiple teachers." Four months seems like an extreme amount of time to adjust to middle school. Obviously those kids haven't had much risk-taking experience!

I met a mother who told me her children, ranging in age from 5 to 13, had only ever attended their home church. "It would just be too traumatic for them to be in a different church, so we'd never consider moving," she told me. There's no greater feeling of taking a risk than walking into an unfamiliar place of worship. When Sondra was 12, we took a year and traveled around the United States in an RV. Each Sunday, Sondra gave a presentation at a different church, looking for sponsors for AIDS orphans in Africa. Some days, we'd find ourselves in a tiny rural congregation where the choir sang traditional hymns. The next week, we'd visit a mega-church with a full rock-and-roll band and high-tech videos. Through that experience alone, Sondra now feels comfortable attending any church service or general meeting. She's experienced the situation with our guidance and now conquers new situations on her own.

Positive risk taking can be as simple as having your daughter enter some contests (no, I don't mean beauty pageants with makeup and flouncy dresses). Every community has contests such as writing a "Why My Dad Is the Best Dad in the World" essay or designing a poster for a new florist shop.

When Trina was nine, a local dentist sponsored a contest for National Dental Health Week. Kids were to make a poster related to brushing teeth. I "assigned" Trina the task of entering the contest. It's been over 25 years, and I still remember her winning slogan, printed over a giant mouth:

> Brush, Brush and dental floss too,
> And no cavities will come to you!

It's not Robert Frost, but it won her a $100 gift certificate for a bookstore.

Entering a contest such as this still requires effort on your part. If you ask your daughter, "Do you want to enter this poster contest?" she'll probably say no. In that case, approach the topic in a different way. Make some root beer floats; bring out the contest rules, some paper, markers, and other supplies; and simply engage your daughter. "I thought would be fun if we work on this poster contest together. What color paper do you want for the background?" After the project is completed, have your daughter help you address the envelope or drop off the project according to the rules. There's a risk in entering, because you may not win. But there's also a chance of winning a prize!

Ever since Sondra was little, I've had her enter contests. Not only do they encourage risk taking but they also teach her valuable skills in creativity and rule-following. She won $1,000 in a short-essay contest sponsored by Burger King. A newspaper ran a contest to have students write why they want to meet a local businessperson of their choice; not only did Sondra win a $1,000 scholarship but her school also received $5,000! We're incredibly proud of her latest prize-winning entry. The Duck Brand Products sponsors a "Duct Tape Dad of the Year" contest. Sondra's second-place essay won her dad a year's supply of duct tape!

Now that Sondra is applying for college scholarships, she's experienced in reading the fine print to meet deadlines and other crucial requirements. Just yesterday we found out she won a $650 scholarship from the Veterans of Foreign Wars, based on a two-minute speech she needed to submit on a CD. Here's her winning entry.

Freedom's Responsibility

Think about all the toothbrushes you've had in your life. Yes, toothbrushes. Stay with me, this will tie in to the theme of "Freedom's Responsibility."

When you were little, you probably had a cute yellow toothbrush with a few soft bristles. Then you advanced to a bright colored toothbrush with a picture of Superman or some other popular cartoon character. As you got older, your toothbrushes got more sophisticated and you probably even tried an electric toothbrush that vibrated and brushed so fast it guaranteed you'd never have cavities again. We take our toothbrushes for granted, just like we take our freedom for granted.

I was born into freedom. My parents chose the hospital where I'd be delivered and from then on it was one freedom after another. Today, if I want to read a censored book like *Of Mice and Men* or protest about my high school dress code, I have that freedom. Like most people, I didn't think about the responsibility that comes with freedom.

That all changed when I was 12 years old and visited a remote island in Uganda. I suddenly found myself in the middle of children who lived without food, without parents, and without freedom. On Bugala Island, 50% of the population has AIDS. This means many children have lost both parents and are living on their own.

On the island, I met Annette, a 12-year-old girl that our family sponsors. We pay $30.00 a month so Annette can live in a children's home, get medical attention and go to school. She spoke English so we were able to have a conversation. I brought her some presents like crayons, colored paper, and some new socks. The six pairs of socks were packed in an ordinary shrink-wrapped piece of plastic. I handed Annette the socks in the shiny bag and she said

"What is this?"

Oh just some socks I answered. She kept looking and touching the package, running her fingers around the plastic. Once again she asked, "What is this?"

I said "Here, I'll open the bag so you can see the socks." With that, I ripped the plastic and handed her the six socks. She ignored the socks and took the plastic bag. Annette held the bag up to her eyes and looked through it. She smelled the plastic and smiled as it crinkled in her hands. Then it hit me . . . . . . she had never seen a plastic bag before. Annette doesn't have the freedom to leave her isolated island where a plastic bag is a novelty.

Returning home, I came across a quote by Dwight Eisenhower. He said "Freedom has its life in the hearts, the actions, and the spirit of men. It must be daily earned and refreshed, or like a flower cut from its life giving roots, it will wither and die." My responsibility is to use my freedom daily in my heart, my actions, and in my spirit.

That's why I knew it was my responsibility to use my freedom to help the children I met in Uganda.

It's easy to say, I'm only 16. Why do I have to be responsible for kids living half way around the world? Because of my freedom I do have responsibility. I began by speaking to youth groups, schools, Kiwanis groups and Rotary clubs, telling them about the children I met in Africa. I stressed that we have a responsibility to help people who don't have the freedom we have.

By raising awareness, I was able to collect over $85,000 for children that I met in Kenya and Uganda.

Because I saw that people were so willing to help, I organized a new project this summer called Fun With A Future. In the past, I raised money which went to help with the children's education, medical attention, and other necessities. Yet I felt a responsibility to give the kids some fun. They had no toys, videos, or even basic balls and bats. So I started speaking at schools, camps, and service clubs, asking for donations. I collected 1,000 Frisbees. I choose the Frisbees because they are durable and groups of kids can play together. Then I collected 10,000 pencils and 5,000 toothbrushes. I choose toothbrushes and pencils because they are items that the kids actually need. The Frisbees supplied the fun. The toothbrushes and pencils supplied items to help the children with their future. That's why I called my project, Fun with a Future.

Responsibility takes many forms; we have the responsibility to vote, to drive safely, and pay taxes. Sometimes responsibility means doing something a bit unusual.... Responsibility can be collecting 5,000 toothbrushes.

Sondra's experience in taking risks by entering coloring contests is paying off in reducing college costs. Now that's a great benefit for Allan and me!

Looking for a great way to give your daughter experience in positive risk taking while you lounge on the couch eating bon-bons? Send her to camp! Having worked in camps for many years, I know firsthand the benefits of the camping experience. In a safe, supportive environment, girls learn to get along with others as well as learning new skills. She'll take risks crawling over logs, kayaking on lakes, and tackling challenging rope courses.

Look at it this way. Trained counselors have to put up with the mosquitoes and hyperactive tweens. You simply need to listen when your daughter regales you with her daring escapades! She'll discover the satisfaction of carrying a backpack up a steep mountain path. Your normally picky eater will wolf down anything served because she's experiencing real hunger. Socially, she'll take on new risks by being in cabin groups with girls she doesn't know. What should she say when a cabin mate shares her thoughts of running away? Separated from their mothers, girls start to rely on their inner resources or find a trusted adult to help. Camp allows girls to experiment with new personalities. I've seen many tween girls come to camp doing anything to be outgoing and popular. Within a few days, they settle comfortably into being who they *really* are. As girls try dirt-bike racing or swinging from giant rope swings, they go away with a go get 'em attitude. After all, if she can navigate through the woods with a GPS system, she can certainly figure out how to switch classrooms in middle school!

To find an accredited camp in your area, check out the American Camping Association at www.aca.org. (Make sure the camp is ACA accredited. That means the camp has passed stringent inspections regarding safety and training procedures.)

Going to camp is an easy and traditional way to take safe risks. Ready for something a little more challenging? (Stay with me—you and your daughter will both benefit from this suggestion.) As your daughter gets to be 11 or 12, she'll probably start thinking about various career possibilities. After progressing past the idea of being a ballerina and a princess as a preschooler, she'll have a few questions concerning her place in the working world. Unfortunately, colleges report that many students select a major based on the popularity of TV shows. For example, your daughter may decide to be a fashion designer after watching *Project Runway*. Your job is to help her see that careers should be based on more than television.

That's where *job shadowing* comes in as a powerful risk-taking activity. Your daughter basically "shadows" someone on the job, observing what he or she does. Job shadowing is a perfect summer activity. Have your daughter read a few books on different careers and select one that interests her. Does she want to work with animals? Call a local veterinarian and see if you and your daughter can come by and observe for an hour. If a vet isn't available, contact a pet store or the humane society. Does a neighbor own a flower shop? See if she'll let you and your daughter come by. Most people are more than willing to share their time with a young person.

One word of caution. At this age, try to have your daughter shadow someone with a slightly "physical" job. It's no fun to observe someone working at a computer. One mother of a budding 11-year-old broadcaster arranged for her daughter to watch her two favorite radio personalities from behind the scenes. They even introduced her on the air and conducted a quick interview.

Sondra had the unusual experience of job-shadowing 55 people across the U.S. When we were taking our yearlong trip around the country, the National Recreation and Park Association asked her to shadow people in recreation-related jobs and write a book about her experiences. She had so much fun that she shadowed people in a variety of careers. She spent the day with Shamu's trainer at SeaWorld, a shoe designer at Nike, a Broadway theater critic, and a photographer at Lands' End. In every case, I simply called up, told them we were in the area, and asked if Sondra could job-shadow an employee. No one ever refused our request.

Look at all the positive risk-taking aspects built into job shadowing:

- Your daughter is in a new environment.
- She's with people she may not know.
- There are sights and smells and activities she's never experienced.

And look at the advantages she gains from job shadowing:

- She meets interesting people.
- She sees firsthand what it takes to work in a particular career.
- She learns to ask appropriate questions.
- She feels "grown-up" being in an adult word.
- She learns to write a thank-you note to the person she shadowed.
- She has great stories to share with the rest of her family!

Parents have told me that the job-shadowing experience gave their daughter insight as well as confidence. How exciting to be able to tell your teacher that you got to help feed the seahorses at the local aquarium! Sondra had the unusual experience of people actually offering her jobs! One person told us, "I'd hire your daughter on the spot. She was so willing to help set up items for the photo shoot, plus she made eye contact and spoke in full sentences. Our college interns don't do that." Sondra gained so much from her job-shadowing experiences that she thinks it should be a required class for high school students.

Sondra says: Walk through any high school cafeteria and you'll hear snippets of conversation such as "I saw *Grey's Anatomy* last night and decided I want to be a doctor" or "I want to be a forensic scientist, like on *CSI!*" Many teens look toward current TV shows for career direction. In recent years, colleges have seen a rise in students wanting to major in interior design because of shows like *Trading Spaces.* Buffalo State College reports an increase in students wanting to major in fashion design because of the popular show *Project Runway.* Elaine Polvines, professor of its fashion textile program, gets three to six calls daily from prospective students. The college has also seen an increase in forensic science majors because of the success of *CSI.*

I think job shadowing should be required for all middle and high school students. This is simply the opportunity for a student to "shadow" someone at her or his job and see what the job is really like. When students do a job shadow, they get a firsthand look at a real job, rather than seeing the job unrealistically portrayed on TV. According to the University of California, Riverside, 50–70 percent of college students change their major at least once. If students did some job shadows, they would have a more realistic idea of which major to take and could avoid wasting time (and money) taking classes they don't need.

I had the unusual opportunity to participate in 55 job shadows across the nation. I stuffed vitamins into a salmon to give to Shamu at SeaWorld. At Nike headquarters, I helped design a new running shoe. I even spent the day shadowing a rocket scientist!

In doing the job shadows, I learned that what some people consider a dream job would bore me. One gym supervisor was so happy with his job scheduling basketball tournaments and wiping sweat off the court. At one time, I thought being a chef would be a great idea. (Wasn't Monica on *Friends* a happy chef?) After spending time with a chef at a Marriott hotel, I changed my mind. He spent 45 minutes teaching me to "smell" different cuts of meat to distinguish which was rotten and which was safe to eat! Then there was the time I wanted to be a veterinarian ... until I fainted as a vet performed a hysterectomy on a cat.

Just don't ask Sondra what she wants to be when she grows up. She had so many amazing job-shadowing experiences, she can't narrow down her choice to just one career!

Just for Fun

Show your daughter that you have a go get 'em attitude, too! Find an activity that is physically challenging for both of you. Do something that gets your adrenaline rushing through your bodies! Allan and I recently tried hang gliding. A small plane pulls the hang glider up to 2,000 feet (which is *really* high!) and then releases the tow cable. You and your trained instructor drift silently through the air. My heart was still pounding several hours after we landed! Does the budget allow you to try parasailing? How about signing up for a kayak trip or river rafting excursion? Join a group of mountain bikers for a rough-and-tumble bike ride. If January 1 is coming up, participate in a Polar Bear Swim on New Year's Day. Show your daughter that appropriate risk taking is fun (after the apprehension wears off). Celebrate afterward with a root beer float!

Chapter 9

How to Help Her Develop Self-Confidence

Looking for a new experience? Feeling brave? Want to see how tween hierarchy works? Volunteer to help in a classroom (not your daughter's!) at school. While it will look like you are helping the teacher, you actually have ulterior motives. Use this opportunity to observe the varying self-confidence levels of the students. Some students boldly stride into a room, knowing they can handle any situation. Others walk in head down, shoulders slouched, wanting nothing more than to disappear in the corner.

Listen as various groups work on a project. You might hear something like this:

Ashley: "Why do we have to do this dumb assignment?"
Monica: "I don't know."
Ashley: "What should we do?"
Alex: "Maybe we should get the poster paper."
Monica: "I guess."
Ashley: "What color should we get? I want pink."
Alex: "Not pink! Monica, what color do you want?"
Monica: "Umm, I don't care."

Monica certainly doesn't feel free to speak up and express her opinion, does she? Now listen in on another group, led by self-assured Leslie.

Leslie: "Okay, guys, we have to make the best poster ever so we can get a good grade. I don't really care about drawing the food pyramid, but that's the assignment, so we'll go with it. Who wants to draw the outline of the pyramid with perfectly straight lines?'
Jenny: "I can do that, I guess."

Leslie: "Actually, Jenny, I think you need to draw the food. You're a good artist. Steven, why don't you draw the outline of the pyramid?"

Steven: "Oh ... Okay."

Leslie: "Good. We need someone to do the research about what we're supposed to eat every day. Melissa, you like research. Why don't you do that?"

Melissa: "I'll get our science book and see if there's information in there."

Leslie: "Good. If everyone does their part, we'll get an A on this project! Oh! I just had a great idea! While you're all working on your assignments, Adam and I will make up a rap song about the food pyramid. I bet we get extra credit!"

You may be laughing, thinking that tweens don't talk like this. Yet I've heard many similar conversations when self-confident tweens work on a project. What gives Leslie the confidence to take control and delegate? (Some people might say she's just plain bossy!) Hard to say. Yet take a look at what she does. While other groups might sit around, wondering what to do, Leslie takes action. She points out that Jenny is a good artist and Melissa likes research. Leslie sees beyond herself and acknowledges the strengths of other students. She feels comfortable stating her opinions, such as "I don't really care about drawing the food pyramid," yet knows it's important to complete the assignment.

As you observe the classroom, listen for students saying things like:

- "I can't be in the play. I'm no good at memorizing."
- "My math is horrible."
- "Can I watch the spelling bee? I don't want to be in it."
- "Do I have to read my report out loud? Can't I just turn it in?"
- "I want to be on the track team, but I'm a slow runner."

Why is it that some tweens like Leslie are so confident and willing to take risks? (Would *you* volunteer to make up a rap song about the food pyramid?) What's the difference between Leslie's self-confidence level and that of Monica, who doesn't want to commit to a certain color of poster paper?

Parents strive to help their children develop self-confidence. We all want our children to eagerly participate in school or volunteer to play goalie on the soccer team. Yet often (well-meaning as we are), parents *undermine* their children's ability to develop self-confidence. If a preschooler runs into a room carrying a glass of water, what's the first thing most parents say? You'll usually hear, "Be careful, you'll spill the water." How about saying, "Susie, it's a good idea to walk when carrying a glass of water"? Why encourage a self-fulfilling prophecy by telling Susie she'll spill the water?

If you don't feel comfortable going to a classroom, simply take your daughter to a local park. Observe the children running, jumping, and climbing over and under the equipment. It's not hard to notice the dare-devils who slide headfirst down the slide and then leap from the hanging bars to begin twirling feverishly on the tire swing. These kids know no fear! Then there are the cautious playground participants. They slowly walk across the shaky wooden bridge. It takes them time to get the courage to slide down the fireman's pole. What makes the difference? I've seen parents watch their 9-year-old on a park playground. As soon as the child starts doing something a tiny bit "dangerous," Mom yells, "Amy, don't climb so high! You'll get hurt!" Now that's building confidence!

In some cases, tween girls ooze self-confidence. When 13-year-old Kelsey was asked, "What one thing would you change about your life?" she answered, "I would make my friends more confident in who they are." Yet in the majority of cases, we had girls answer our survey with statements like this:

- "My friends all know what to do when we're in a group. I feel awkward."
- "I wish I could have more confidence. Yesterday I was scared to ask the school librarian how to find a book."
- "I'm not athletic and I hate being in front of people. My friend wanted me to try out for the school play, but I'd die if I had to be on stage."
- "My parents don't help me do anything. I wanted to try out for choir, and my mom said I wasn't a good singer. Then I wanted to be on the soccer team, and my dad said I wasn't athletic enough."

Let's look at some ways to help your daughter gain self-confidence in herself and her abilities.

Be a positive role model. How often as adults do we say, "I'll never be able to make that presentation next week." Or, "I wish I knew how to use this new computer program. I'll never learn." Your daughter needs to see a mom with a can-do attitude. Girls gain coping skills by hearing her mom say, "The boss asked me to give a PowerPoint presentation next week. I've never done it, but I found this great magazine article that has some tips, so I'll give it a try." (Or do what most moms do and ask your 12-year-old to help you with the PowerPoint presentation!)

If things don't work out, keep a positive attitude. Your daughter learns so much from seeing you take on an unfamiliar situation. I took a risk and auditioned for a part in a community theater play. I didn't get the lead (or even a minor part), but I did let my daughter see me stepping out of my comfort zone and making the best of the situation. While I wasn't headed for Broadway, I did become involved with the theater by volunteering as box office manager.

Let your daughter see your resiliency in overcoming a challenge. I remember a situation where I boldly stepped into a job that was way beyond my experience. I know how to sell myself at job interviews. Walk right in, give a firm handshake, and then dazzle the interviewer with my wit and confidence. Studies say that the decision to hire someone is often made within the first 30 seconds of the interview. People have offered me jobs within 25 seconds because I know how to make a great first impression. Here's the catch: I get hired for jobs way beyond my experience and relevant skills. Impressed with my interview savvy, employers offer me jobs better suited for, say, someone with the experience and relevant skills.

So there I was, newly hired as the children's director of a large church. The hiring committee overlooked the fact that I had little Sunday School experience and certainly no idea how to teach children. But I sure knew how to conduct myself at a job interview!

My first assignment involved teaching a class of third-graders until their regular Sunday School teacher returned from maternity leave. Glancing through the curriculum (why bother to thoroughly read a lesson plan?), I noticed that they were studying the Ten Commandments. "Thou shalt have no graven images" caught my attention.

On Sunday morning, my new students walked into their Sunday School room to find a veritable building center for graven images. "We're going to build graven images!" I announced in the same perky voice used during my successful job interview. These 8-year-olds had no idea what a graven image was, but they eagerly set out constructing structures with toilet paper rolls and empty boxes. "The bigger the better!" I announced. Rolls of duct tape helped hold five-foot structures together. Giant plastic wiggle eyes adding intriguing personalities to idols made from beach balls and milk jugs. Kids had paint on their "Sunday" clothes and smiles on their faces. The room looked like the corporate warehouse for Graven Images, Inc.

Being inexperienced in teaching, I never bothered to explain the relationship of the Ten Commandments to their young lives. Who had time for a meaningful lesson when there were life-size graven images to construct? The hour-long class passed quickly, with children actively engaged the whole time. Isn't that what quality teaching is all about?

Suddenly I noticed parents arriving to pick up their children. I knew I had to get some sort of Biblical message to the students. "Listen carefully," "I said. "The Bible says we *should not* worship graven images." The class stared at me, graven images precariously swaying in the background. "So ... let's destroy these images!"

With that, all 15 kids began ripping apart the graven images. Boxes toppled after being punched, beach balls got popped, and boxes covered in wet paint ended up staining the carpet. Parents walked in to see frenzied children yelling, "Destroy! Destroy!" accompanied by karate kicks to the graven images. One father got hit in the head with a wiggle-eyed milk jug. Another girl cried because she had planned to take her life-size statue home—until it was crushed by an enthusiastic classmate.

Parents with stunned faces grabbed their children and swept them away to safety. After several phone calls from parents the following day, the pastor suggested I stick to having my class color pictures in the future.

Mother-Daughter Mini-Activity

Select a new hobby, class, or activity that neither of you has done before. Attempt something new together. Maybe take a tap dance class, or learn how to make a soufflé. Read a book together on a topic you normally wouldn't select. It can be as simple as taking a free one-hour class in scrapbooking at a local craft store. Discuss with your daughter what it feels like to take a risk and try something new.

One of the hardest ways to be a positive role model is when it comes to our body image. How often do we mutter, "I can't believe how tight these pants are. I really need to lose some weight"? Naturally our daughters are standing next to us as we contort our bodies and suck in our stomachs in a valiant effort to look thinner in the mirror—a valiant effort that doesn't work! You've probably seen the Campaign for Real Beauty by Dove. These "normal"-size women appear in print ads and TV commercials wearing only their underwear. (That's brave!) Dove commissioned a global study that found that only 2 percent of women around the world describe themselves as beautiful. The Campaign for Real Beauty encourages woman to be healthy and satisfied with their bodies. The campaign ties in with "Uniquely ME!" a program designed to help girls develop high self-esteem. The website www.campaignforrealbeauty.com also offers a free downloadable self-esteem-building mother-daughter workbook called "True You."

The next time you have some free time with your daughter, bring out the glue, scissors, and old magazines. Work together making a collage, asking your daughter to cut out pictures showing positive and negative body images. Ask her why she selected each picture and how it relates to the way she looks.

A study by Mediafamily.org found that 40 percent of 9- and 10-year-olds have tried to lose weight and that half of 13-year-olds are dissatisfied with their body. Make a conscious effort to emphasize healthy eating habits and exercise. Try some of these tips:

• With this age group, you still have the ability to control what they eat at home. This sounds obvious, but why not stop buying junk food? When kids can't find chips in the cupboard, they'll eat an apple if they get hungry enough. Having worked at camps for many years, I'm always surprised at how quickly kids change their eating habits. A 10-year-old who is used to eating doughnuts for breakfast and fries for lunch, washing everything down with pop, suddenly finds herself without junk food at camp. By the end of the week, this girl is snacking on carrot sticks and drinking milk or water—because that's what's available.

- Place less emphasis on food. Okay, maybe this is just my pet peeve, but do we have to center every special event, meeting, or soccer game around food? Is it necessary at breakfast to talk about what you're having for dinner? A matter-of-fact statement such as, "Here's some cheese and grapes if you want an after-school snack," is fine. We became friends with a Dutch family visiting the United States for the first time. The mom bluntly told me, "One of the biggest surprises is how often Americans snack. I see moms picking up children after school, and they have snacks available in the car. Then there's another snack before dinner and then a bedtime snack. No wonder your kids are overweight. There's nothing wrong with kids being hungry once in a while!" She went on to tell me that at 53 years old, she had never eaten in a car! (I made sure to hide the evidence of food wrappers tossed on my car seat when we went for a drive!)

- Provide food choices, but in a low-key way. One mom casually asks her daughter, "Do you want your broccoli raw or steamed?" That's all. There's no discussion about wanting French fries or hating broccoli or why can't they have macaroni and cheese or why they have to eat disgusting vegetables and so on.

- Family meals are important for creating a strong family. According to a 2005 study by Columbia University, teenagers who eat with their families at least five times a week are more likely to get better grades and much less likely to have substance abuse problems. A University of Michigan study found that "mealtime is the single strongest predictor of better achievement and fewer behavioral problems. The importance of mealtime is far more powerful than time spent in school studying, sports, and art activities."

- *What* you eat is not as important as *how* you eat. A simple soup-and-salad dinner where everyone casually sits around and shares the funniest thing that happened in the last week is far more valuable than a labor-intensive gourmet meal with family members eating in silence. Ever watch those scenes in *Desperate Housewives* where Bree makes a leg of lamb dinner with sautéed baby vegetables served with a wine sauce? The food is delicious, yet the family is so dysfunctional that the meal usually ends with someone throwing a plate or screaming at another family member. When Sondra was 11, we had finished eating dinner one night when my husband announced, "Dessert will be served in 15 minutes. Please come back to the table for a unique dessert experience." Naturally we were curious at what delightful dessert we'd enjoy, so we eagerly returned in 15 minutes. Instead of seeing a traditional pie or gooey brownie, Allan had an apple on the table. One single Red Delicious apple. "Let's take a close look at this apple," he said. "We take apples for granted, but they really are quite special." Allan went on to have us each use a cloth to shine the apple. We looked at our reflections in the apple, smelled the apple, and discussed the apple's shape. Next, Allan peeled a small portion of the apple so we could taste just the skin. Using the peeler, we each tried to peel a continuous strip of skin. Allan pulled out a tape measure so we could measure each piece. Allan had Sondra twist the stem, saying the letter of the alphabet with each turn. When the stem twisted off at the letter G, that meant her first baby would have a name starting with G. When it came time to cut the apple in half, Allan cut it width-wise, not from the stem to the bottom. With a flourish, he displayed the two cut pieces to show a "star" inside, formed by the seeds. It still wasn't time to eat the apple. Oh, no. We had to count the seeds and talk about where to plant the seeds in the hope of starting a backyard apple orchard. By this time, Sondra and I were salivating, wanting to take a bite out of the apple! Finally Allan cut the apple. First he cut a piece in very thin slices, then had us compare the taste with thicker slices. Who knew eating an apple could turn into a whole "Apple Extravaganza"? We could have gulped down a high-calorie chocolate cake while watching TV. Instead, our family enjoyed time together—and gained a whole new appreciation for the lowly apple!

- Incorporate exercise into everyday routines. When Sondra was in fourth grade, we'd occasionally ride bikes the two miles to school. Naturally this meant two extra trips for me, since I'd ride home alone, then go back to the school in the afternoon. (Not that the exercise hurt!) Other days, she'd take the bus to school and I'd meet her after school to walk home together. I still remember feeling exhilarated while holding her hand as she talked nonstop about how the substitute teacher didn't know where the bathroom pass was located and Kelly almost wet her pants. You don't get that kind of information from Katie Couric on the evening news! Another mom would park three blocks from her daughter's dance class. Together they'd walk to class while Mom continued walking around the area until class ended. See? She was being a positive role model! Does your daughter want a trip to the mall on Saturday morning? Offer to take her, knowing you can incorporate exercise before shopping. Simply say, "Yes, I'll take you to the mall, as long as we leave 30 minutes before the mall opens to do some brisk mall walking." Sure, she'll complain, but simply repeat, "Yes, I'll take you to the mall, as long as we leave 30 minutes before the mall opens to do some brisk mall walking." It's her choice!

We may not even be aware how often our daughters look to us as role models. When collecting surveys of tween girls for this book, we asked the question, "Who do you go to when you find yourself in a situation you don't now how to handle?" The majority of girls answered "My mom." It's obvious we still play an important role in the lives of our daughters. By being strong role models, our daughters gain self-confidence.

Another way to help our daughters grow into self-confident women is by keeping praise in perspective. There's a tendency for moms to applaud every action their daughters make. There's no need to clap and cheer if your 10-year-old puts her napkin on her lap at dinner. That's expected behavior. Children soon that learn they can do almost anything and their parents will automatically give a standing ovation—but that praise soon loses its meaning. Of course you want to give positive feedback, but at least make it realistic.

We had a mother in our preschool class that gushed with wonder if her daughter breathed. One day she looked at her daughter's collage, consisting of one cotton ball and two pieces of felt glued to a piece of paper. "Oh, Amy," she gushed. "This is the most amazing piece of artwork I've seen. Look at what a lovely collage you made. You are so artistic! Let's go home and put it up on the wall in a special place of honor." This 4-year-old was certainly capable of making a collage beyond three items glued to paper. In class, Amy consistently needed reinforcement for what she did. She'd ask "Teacher, do you like my picture?" "Didn't I do a good job making a tower with the blocks?" Instead of participating in an activity for her own enjoyment, she needed the approval of others.

A few years later in fifth grade, this mom continued to give enthusiastic praise for all of Amy's minor accomplishments. As Amy prepared to audition for the school talent show, her mother said, "Amy, you are the very best singer in this whole school. Your voice is like an angel. You'll get in the talent show because you have such an amazing singing voice." Well, let's just say Amy's voice wasn't all that angelic in quality, and she didn't get in the talent show. Amy became more withdrawn, unsure how to handle realistic situations in comparison to her mother's lavish praise. She had to reconcile who she really was with her mother's unrealistic expectations. Is it any wonder Amy lacked self-confidence?

Let's look at realistic praise and over-the-top, too-good-to-be-true praise. Here are some examples of the latter kind:

- "Jessica, you were such a standout at the dance recital. None of the other girls could dance as well as you. Let's look at getting you into Julliard."
- "Sarah, I've never read such a great essay! Your teacher is sure to give you an A, because it's so creative and well written. This is college-level material!"
- "When it comes to art, you are amazing! I'm getting this painting framed, because it deserves to be hung in the living room. It won't be long before your artwork is sold in galleries around the world!"
- "Oh Megan . . . look at this science poster you made! They say girls aren't good in science, but you are the best! I think you'll be the first woman on the moon because you are so talented in science!"

Now let's try some realistic praise:

- "Emma, I see your studying has paid off. Your history grade has gone up from a C to a B. Looks like that extra effort with your study group is working."
- "Thanks for cleaning the kitchen, Hannah. I appreciate that you wiped down the counters after emptying the dishwasher."
- "Congratulations on your 'most improved' soccer award, Emily! It was hard joining the team midseason, yet your extra effort helped you get caught up with the rest of the team."

The first set of comments simply makes grandiose claims about a girl's abilities. The second set contains realistic comments that point out exactly what she's accomplished.

Megan, age 11: "My mom was constantly telling me how smart I was. Even if I got a bad grade on a test, she'd blame it on the teacher. I had this feeling I was *really* smart. Then I went to middle school. I saw I wasn't all that smart. It shocked me!"

Mother-Daughter Mini-Activity

Many adults agonize over writing a résumé to list their accomplishments and jobs. Give your daughter an insight into this process by helping her write a personal résumé. List her accomplishments and skills, such as:

- Can swim underwater two lengths of the pool
- Knows multiplication tables up to "11s"
- Can keep younger brother entertained with games and activities
- Knows how to make three types of pop-up cards
- Winner of third-grade spelling bee

She may not have a list of job experiences, but she will have a realistic list of her capabilities and accomplishments. Repeat this process yearly so you both have a record of her new skills.

I started helping Sondra put a résumé together when she was seven. She proudly recorded her skills at tree climbing, bike riding, and doing cartwheels. The résumé gave her tangible evidence of her talent and capabilities. Today at 17, she has no problem putting together a résumé for a part-time job or college scholarship.

When girls have realistic knowledge about who they are, there's less chance they'll fixate on unrealistic expectations. In one of our surveys, we asked girls, "What would you change about yourself?" Eleven-year-old Jessica answered, "I would make myself a famous pop star instead of a pop star wannabe." In the book *Fame Junkies* by Jake Halpren, 43 percent of teen girls said their number-one career goal was celebrity assistant. They felt that just being close to a celebrity would give them rock star status. In a survey of 653 middle school students, when given an option to become either stronger, smarter, famous, or beautiful, boys in the survey chose fame almost as often as intelligence, and girls chose it more often. Why not start now by encouraging your daughter to gain "fame" through developing self-confidence and practical skills that last a lifetime?

Another way to help your daughter develop self-confidence is by letting her solve age-appropriate problems. As mothers, we have a tendency to be "fixers." We want to fix everything possible to make sure our daughters have wonderful lives. Teacher too strict? Get your daughter switched to another class. Didn't get invited to the major birthday party for Katie, the most popular girl in the universe? Throw an all-out extravaganza for your daughter—and make sure Katie isn't invited. Daughter got cut from the elite soccer team? Use your retirement fund to hire Olympic-caliber soccer coaches and start your own league (of course, your daughter is guaranteed a spot on the team).

Okay, those are extreme examples, but mothers do what we can so our daughters are able to live happy, carefree lives. In reality, we're teaching our daughter that Mom will handle any situation. What happens when your daughter has to make decisions on her own? Experts have a name for overprotective mothers and fathers: "helicopter parents." These parents continually hover over their children, influencing every aspect of their sons' and daughters' lives. Some businesses share stories of parents actually coming along to job interviews with their 20-something children!

Self-confident children have the skills and internal strength to solve problems. Your 9-year-old daughter may not have solved the problem of global warming (not yet anyway), but she can solve the problem of having to stay inside for recess because of her messy desk.

Sondra came out of the womb declaring, "I can do it myself!" As she struggled to dress herself as a toddler, I wanted to assist by adjusting the neck opening in her top or snapping her pants. Instead, I forced myself to wait. Usually this produced a gleeful "I dressed myself, Mom!" Other times, if I saw the task truly was too difficult, I'd wait until just before the point of frustration hit and then ask, "Can I help you just a little bit?"

This was especially helpful when, as a 5-year-old, Sondra decided to make swimsuits for poor people. (I'm not sure where she got that idea!) She had various pieces of felt, which she attempted to sew together on the sewing machine. Sondra knew how to use the machine using cotton fabric, but the felt was simply too unwieldy. It was only after I let her experience some frustration with the felt that she suggested using a lighter-weight fabric. She solved the problem by herself, producing a beaming child saying, "Guess what, Mom? Felt isn't good to sew on a machine." Not an earth-shatteringly profound statement, but an experience that helped her with problem-solving abilities.

So, the next time your daughter has a problem, step back and let her work on it. Casually suggest she make a list of three or four options to solve the problem. If she struggles or gets frustrated, give her time to work through the situation. (Obviously this applies only to age-appropriate problems like not getting a new American Girl doll for her birthday or ending up with only a small part in the school play. If your daughter is facing extreme bullying or is in danger, your role as a mother is to step in and take over.)

Problem solving arises in everyday situations. Does your daughter want to have her hair highlighted at a fancy salon that's over your budget? Have her call a few beauty colleges and check out their rates. Can she look in the paper for salons offering coupons or first-time customer discounts? What can she do to earn some money to pay part of the cost? Encourage her to use creative thinking to afford the beauty salon fee.

One teacher assigned the usual homework assignment of constructing a model of the solar system—with no Styrofoam balls allowed! Parents actually called, complaining that their children couldn't possibly complete the assignment without Styrofoam balls. The wise teacher told parents to relax and let the children find a solution. Students did, including one who made a model of Jupiter and Saturn from a combination of glue and dryer lint!

How about a root beer float problem-solving activity? Next time you and your daughter want to drink a float, have her do an experiment. Is there any difference between adding ice cream to root beer versus pouring root beer over the ice cream? Which produces more foam? (See? Those root beer floats are wonderful for teaching all sorts of life lessons!)

Sondra says: Several years ago I saw a brochure for a private girl's school. It showed picturesque ivy-covered brick buildings with a lake in the background. Girls sat on wrought-iron benches, dressed in plaid skirts with freshly pressed white blouses peeking out from their crested blue vests. Pictures of the library highlighted polished oak shelves stacked between ceiling-high stained-glass windows. It looked straight out of Oxford. "Average class size is one teacher for every six girls!" the brochure exclaimed. "Strong emphasis on academics!" "A place where every girl is accepted!" Looking at the brochure, I knew this was a school I wanted to attend.

Many hours of testing, interviews, and filling out scholarship forms found me with an acceptance letter. I was in! Even though I didn't know anyone at the school, my confidence was high. Self-esteem had never been a problem for me. Hey! I could walk into any room, with any group of people and feel right at home. I knew making strong eye contact and asking people about themselves was the way to be in control of the situation. My parents always taught me to tackle new challenges with enthusiasm.

When I arrived on the first day of school, I quickly saw that white knee socks played second place to Jimmy Choo shoes. Blouses were unbuttoned to show off Tiffany necklaces. Girls could name off the latest fashion designers faster than naming the last three presidents. One dad made a yearly contribution of one million dollars to the school.

For the first few weeks of school, I kept a low profile and tried to blend in. When other girls complained about an excess of homework, I joined in the groaning. But in the back of my mind, I thought, "It only took 15 minutes. What's the big deal?" When they snickered at a freshman's new haircut, I commented, "She must think she's living in the '80s to think she can pull that off." During class, the "cool" thing was to slouch in your chair, arms crossed, and look bored, no matter how engaging the teacher was. I began slouching. The more I slouched, the worse I felt. My self-esteem was leaving as I tried to fit in with the culture of this close-knit girl's school. I quickly figured out that if the girls cut each other down, then they also cut me down when I wasn't around. Would I ever fit in? I didn't even know where to buy Jimmy Choos.

Without realizing it, I was changing who I was in order to fit in with the perfect girls on the perfect brochure. I had come to the school to be challenged academically, but instead I found myself challenged to know the address of the latest designer boutique.

Just as my self-esteem was sliding downhill, I happened to pick up my well-read copy of *Anne of Green Gables*. Anne Shirley didn't care what other people thought! She never apologized for who she was. I vowed to make a change. I wore my hair in a casual ponytail instead of having every hair moussed in place. Anne Shirley was an excellent student, so I began paying attention in class. I even answered questions, ignoring the sneers from the other girls. My teachers were thrilled to have a student participate, and I saw how creative they were in their teaching styles. Teachers challenged me to think about Homer and Shakespeare instead of thinking about the latest issue of *Cosmo*.

With the help of *Anne of Green Gables* and my teachers, my self-esteem soon got up to my normal take-charge level. I finished the year with strong academic skills and strong self-esteem. That self-esteem lead me to transfer to another school—where no one snickered when I carried around my copy of *Anne of Green Gables*.

> *A mother and librarian in Wisconsin:* "People come to me at the reference desk because they are having problems finding the information they need. I'm ready to help. At home, I'm ready to help also. The problem is, I help too much. I see now that my 12-year-old is so easily frustrated because I've always bailed her out of every situation. If she was late with a book report, I'd ask the teacher for an extension. When she didn't make the A Squad in gymnastics, I switched her to another gymnastics school so she wouldn't feel bad seeing her friends in the top program. I've worked overtime to pay for her cell phone and designer jeans. Now, when I want to let her solve some of her own problems, it's too overwhelming. She doesn't have basic problem-solving skills."

Here's a unique way to help your daughter develop problem solving skills: Get her involved in craft projects! Think about all the decisions that arise when making arts-and-crafts projects. What color paper should I use for this flower? How can I make a turret for my cardboard castle? What can I do to get the antlers to attach to my moose puppet? This frame is too big for my picture—what can I do?

These small decisions help girls build the basis for solving more complex problems later on in life. Craft projects are open-ended and freeform. If your daughter wants to make a pop-up card with a three-eyed monster, let her! The world needs more three-eyed monsters. There's no pressure to create a masterpiece, so girls can make their own decisions. How can she make pink paint if all she has is red and white paint? Often, as girls try to solve problems, the results can be frustrating. Remember when you tried to deal with the class bully? It was scary and uncomfortable to find ways of dealing with the situation. With crafts, however, the problems are easier to manage. Children gain confidence in their problem-solving skills by starting on a smaller scale.

When Sondra was younger, she watched very little TV. Instead we worked on a variety of craft projects. (I confess, I let her use a glue gun when she was four.) By the time she was eight, Sondra felt comfortable building doll houses with a hammer and drill, sewing costumes on the sewing machine, and decorating pillowcases with fabric crayons and an iron. Oh yes, she wrote her first craft book, *Craft Fun with Sondra*, before her ninth birthday.

Today, as a teenager involved in theater, her problem-solving and craft-making skills come in handy for school plays. Last week a drama teacher pulled Sondra out of history class to ask, "We're stuck! How do we make some abstract, freeform trees for the set of *A Midsummer Night's Dream*?" Sondra came up with a great papier-mâché solution. A few weeks later, the director was stumped about how to make the special angel for the top of the tree in *It's a Wonderful Life*. Sondra used crafting wire, foil, and wire to create an angel similar to the one in the beloved holiday movie. She's learned to think of various solutions when problems come up.

Help your daughter gain problem-solving skills with a few craft projects. Today she'll figure out what to use for antennas on her clay bug. Tomorrow she'll figure out how to solve world peace. In the words of Abraham H. Maslow, "If the only tool you have is a hammer, you tend to see every problem as a nail."

Sondra says: My dad never had the idea that I should only do "girly" things. He taught me how to throw a football. (I actually joined the boys' football team in middle school!) He gave me a full-size tool set for my 11th birthday. He'd involve me when he repaired a roof or fixed the washing machine.

Recently, my theatre class was building a set for a production. The girls were all painting the set, and the boys were using power tools to help build a stairway. Of course, all the boys were trying to show off that they knew what they were doing will all the "manly" tools. One guy, who had a tendency to be a know-it-all, was attempting to screw a brace to some wood, but obviously had no clue how to do it. I confidently walked over and asked, "Do you need some help?" He quickly responded with, "No, it's just that this drill doesn't have enough power, I'm going to go find one that does." The drill had the power—he just didn't know how to use it. By the time he got back, I had expertly done the job! (Okay, I like to show off at times also!)

Another time I was hanging out with a guy friend working on his motorcycle. He asked me to hand him a socket wrench and proceeded to describe what it looked like. By the time he finished the explanation, I already had the wrench and demonstrated to him how to use it. The simple skills my dad gave me have instilled confidence that there is nothing out of my realm to do. Because of him, I have confidence that I can mow a lawn, make basic repairs, and change a tire on my car.

The next time your daughter has a problem, give her these tools to come up with a solution.

- Be specific about the problem. Is it true that "Everybody hates me" or is it that "Haley said my jeans were dorky"?
- Ask why the problem occurred. Did your daughter snub a friend in the cafeteria in favor of a more popular girl? Did your daughter forget to study for a test she failed?
- List possible solutions. Could your daughter take an extra dance class in order to qualify to dance in *The Nutcracker*? What if your daughter got a job as a mother's helper to earn money for her iPod?
- Ask for help if needed. Can Mom or Dad come up with some ideas? Could a teacher suggest an extra-credit project to raise your daughter's English grade?
- Take action. It's all too easy to complain about bad grades, few friends, or lack of talent. Help your daughter take one corrective piece of action to try to solve the problem. If the first plan fails, go on to plan #2.
- Help your daughter face reality. Some problems can't be solved. Her annoying 6-year-old brother is a part of the family and too young for boarding school. She can't wear jeans to school, because the rules require uniforms. Sometimes a strong "Life isn't always fair" is just the dose of reality your daughter needs.

By following these steps, your daughter will gain realistic self-confidence as she learns to solve problems. And we all know, life is not problem-free!

> *A mother of a 12-year-old:* "When my daughter entered middle school, I saw she needed a crash course in problem solving. I'd protected her from any type of frustration and conflict. She didn't have any coping skills, and boy, did she need coping skills in middle school! She also lacked self-confidence because she expected me to deal with parents, teachers, and friends to make her life easy. I had to force myself to step back and let her take on some challenges. It's hard, and she cries when I don't bail her out of problems. Yet slowly but surely she's getting more assertive and confident as she navigates through middle school and solving problems that come along."

Just for Fun

Give your daughter a problem to solve. A fun problem, that is. Set up a situation such as: "Sydney, here is $25. Would you plan a fun Saturday afternoon for us?" Help your daughter look in the paper for special events or ask a relative for ideas. Would $25 stretch far enough to go horseback riding, eat lunch at a fancy tea room, and buy new earrings? She'll gain self-confidence learning to budget time and money. If you don't want to incorporate money, ask her to plan a no-cost mother-daughter activity. You could pack a picnic lunch together and visit a park, or go to a free outdoor concert. This gives a great starting point for telling her how proud you are she worked on a "problem" and came up with a solution.

Chapter 10

Three Guidelines for a Strong Mother-Daughter Relationship

Walk through any bookstore or Google "tweens," and you'll see thousands of tips, newsletters, books, and quotes from experts on the amazingly complex world of raising tweens. To save you hours of reading, this chapter focuses on three basic guidelines that should help you survive your daughter's preteen years with some semblance of sanity.

GUIDELINE #1: YOU ARE A MOTHER, NOT A BEST FRIEND

Carole, a preschool teacher in Seattle: "I wish someone would tell me what to do when my daughter gets upset when I set some rules. She tells me mothers of her friends aren't so strict. I just feel she needs some guidelines, but then she rants and raves about what a mean mother I am. Then she won't talk to me and gives me dirty looks. Of course, I feel bad when she seems to hate me."

Wouldn't it be great if everyone thought we were witty, creative, and a wonderful friend? Wouldn't it be great if our tween daughters thought we were witty, creative, and a wonderful mother? Carole obviously has good intentions, yet lets her feelings get in the way of dealing with her daughter.

It's hard when we try to be good mothers and our daughters make us feel awful. This was evident when I recently watched a popular talk show on overindulged children. The program had me yelling at the on-screen guests, "Your kids don't have to like you!" One teenager demanded so many designer clothes that her mother had to work three jobs to pay the bills. Their home was refinanced twice, and their credit card bills topped $40,000. The mom said, "I want my daughter to be happy and like me, so I buy her anything she wants."

Obviously, that's an extreme situation designed to promote television ratings, but many mothers find themselves in a similar, not-so-drastic position. One mother, an administrative assistant in Kentucky, summed it up like this: "She's my only daughter. I love going shopping with her. If I don't buy her what she wants, she pouts. Then I feel bad. So I buy the item in hopes she'll talk to me again."

Both of the above mothers have a deep desire to be good parents. They also have a deep desire to be liked by their daughters. Yet if you look at the situation on a practical level, both moms are reinforcing their daughter's negative behavior. The scenario goes like this:

1. Little Suzy wants a designer purse.
2. Mom says the purse is too expensive.
3. Little Suzy stops talking to mom.
4. Mom buys the purse.
5. Little Suzy talks to mom for a few days.
6. Mom feels good about the mother-daughter relationship.
7. Suzy decides she needs a new coat to go with the purse.
8. Mom says Suzy already has two coats.
9. Little Suzy gets upset and stops talking to mom.
10. Mom buys the coat.

Do you see the pattern? Daughters soon know all they have to do is pout and give the silent treatment in order to get what they want.

As mothers, it is more important to set limits and model healthy communication skills than to be "best buddies" with our daughters. Have you ever watched the out-of-control children on the hit show *Supernanny*? Mothers on the show usually say, "I was worried my child wouldn't like me if I set rules." (This is after their child has just pulled their hair and spit on them.) Children develop a sense of security knowing that adults are providing boundaries and limits.

> *Jo Rae, a salesperson and writer:* "As part of the mother-daughter relationship, you don't give up the rules or high standards you have previously set. You do, however, remember your own insecurities and how difficult it was to be a self-confident person around peers who you perceive have advantages over you."

Sondra says: As I look back over my loooong life of 17 years, I see that my mom and I do many things that friends do, like riding bikes, doing craft projects, and filling up my costume box. Yet I always know she's Mom, not my best friend. I had a friend named Ashley whose mom always took her to get facials or manicures. Her mom would say, "Ashley, let's have a girl's day out and go shopping and then go to an afternoon at the spa." Ashley really didn't want to go, but her mom kept saying it was fun to be like friends when getting a manicure or pedicure. Ashley actually felt guilty not wanting to be friends with her mom!

All too often, mothers fear saying no to their preteens because they'll hear, "If you don't let me go to the movies, I won't be your friend." You have your own friends. Besides, why would you want to be friends with someone who can't drive and goes days without brushing her teeth, anyway? Mothers don't need to earn their daughter's friendship to be seen as a cool mom. Dr. Michael Thompson, a clinical child psychologist and the author of *Raising Cain* (Ballantine, 2000), says, "No 11-year-old thinks their parents are cool. Cool is an attribute awarded by a peer group. It is developmentally odd when a kid of 12 or 13 says it" (36). So let's stop worrying about being cool and concern ourselves with being a parent.

At times, it's oh-so-easy to start acting like a preteen yourself, yelling, "I don't care if you don't like me. Some day when I'm in a nursing home, you'll feel guilty for treating me this way." Then, of course, your daughter screams, you yell louder, the dog hides under the bed, and the newlyweds next door vow never to have children. The next time you find yourself in a shouting match, do the reverse. The louder your daughter yells, the softer you speak. Once again it shows you are in control. (Not that you aren't screaming inside!) Try bringing out the ice cream and root beer and saying, "Things are getting heated. Let's have a root beer float while we talk about this situation in a semicalm way."

Sondra says: It's true, my mom and I have a good relationship. Sure, we get upset at each other at times. It never lasts long, though. I don't want my mom to be my friend. Friends are supposed to be your own age. (No offense, Mom, but you are getting some gray hairs!) I do have fun with my mom, though not in the same way that I have fun with my friends. It would feel weird to have my mom try to win my "friendship." I look to her for companionship and support, not for someone to hang out with at the mall. My mom's rules are sort of an algebraic equation, like, "Do this, and this will happen. Don't do this, and this will happen." It's up to me to make the choice and then accept the consequences. The one thing I know is that my mom will follow through on what she says. While I don't always like it, I know she's consistent in doing what she says she'll do. Friends aren't always consistent! I have a friend who would tell me she knew she could get her way with her mom. Her mom would tell her to do homework before going on IM. But my friend just IM'd all the time, because her mom never checked her homework. It was obvious my friend didn't have much respect for her mom.

Being a mother and not a best friend means understanding our daughters are not as sophisticated as the media portray. One mother called it "unearned sophistication":

> "My 11-year-old daughter likes horses and sports, not boys. We've had many talks about sex and dating, so I assumed she understood the

concept. One day, after reading a teen magazine, she asked, 'Mom, this article talks about going to bed with a guy. Why would I want to go to bed with a guy? I like sleeping alone." She had no idea that sleeping together usually equated with sex. I got brave and asked some of her friends if they knew what it meant to sleep with a guy. One or two rolled their eyes in disgust, while the others had no idea what the phrase meant. I see my daughter and her friends aren't as sophisticated and world-savvy as we assume. It's so easy to assume they are these mini Britney Spears when they are still innocent girls."

The mother went on to say that she planned to keep her daughter involved in age-appropriate activities, even if the media said 11-year-olds should wear sexy clothing and swoon over boys. That's where being a mother, not a friend, plays a crucial role in your daughter's development.

Sondra says: In middle school, there was a whole group of girls that thought they were so sophisticated. Their mothers kind of went along with the whole "I'm grown up" idea. The moms would buy them skimpy clothes and thought it was so cute when their daughters had boyfriends. Some moms even encouraged boy-girl parties. I'd watch these girls at school getting all excited about playing dodge ball. It showed they still were young on the inside, but had to play this "I'm too cool" role because their parents didn't set limits.

A 12-year-old from Memphis had this to say about her mom acting "like a mom":

"My mom used to read to me every night when I was little. For the last few years, she stopped. Last month my mom bought me one of those Chicken Soup books written for girls my age. My mom said we would start reading it together every night before I went to bed. I thought it was a babyish idea. My mom said we should try it for a week. Now I really like it when she reads to me. We're going to pick out another book and read it together when we get done with this one."

It would have been much easier for her mom to say, "Okay, if you don't want to read together, I understand." Instead, a mother acting like a mother now enjoys a special reading time with her daughter.

Katilia, a program coordinator for teens in Nebraska, sums it up by saying, "Always have an open relationship with your daughter. Keep structure and consistency with rules and consequences for breaking rules. You want to develop a close relationship with your child without them thinking you are their peer."

If you want some more practical parenting tips on dealing with tweens, subscribe to "The One Minute Parent" (www.teenfrontier.com). This free e-mail newsletter by Barbara McRae gives many easy-to-implement ideas.

GUIDELINE #2: REINFORCE POSITIVE BEHAVIOR

Remember the last time your daughter played cooperatively with a sibling? Did you hold your breath, waiting for a fight over the video game? Or did you make a point of telling the two children you noticed they were getting along? When our children are preschoolers, it's easy to say, "Jenny, you and Zach are playing so nicely with the Legos." We forget that older children respond to positive feedback also. After all, if your boss mentions she appreciated the extra graphs you included in the monthly report, won't you continue to add graphs?

It just takes a few phrases such as:

- "Sara, you're following the rules asking permission to watch TV."
- "Hey! I saw how you helped your sister with her homework. She really looks up to you."
- "Megan, I could see how hard you tried this afternoon at memorizing the multi-plication tables."

Notice that those comments are realistic praise. There's no need to gush over your 10-year-old because she put toothpaste on her toothbrush. Effective positive reinforcement helps your child know that what she is doing is appropriate.

When Sondra was a toddler, I'd frequently reinforce positive behavior by saying, "Sondra, you worked hard putting all the puzzle pieces back in the box when you were done playing. I think I'll call Daddy and tell him." She beamed as I placed the call and relayed her great feat of toy cleanup. Naturally her dad would then talk to her on the phone, congratulating her once again on the way she put the puzzle away. We've come a long way from putting puzzle pieces away, but I still try to reinforce positive behavior whenever I can.

Sondra says: Yes, my mom gives me lots of positive feedback, that's true. One day at lunch, she put a fortune cookie in my lunch bag. I casually cracked it open to find a handwritten "fortune" that said, "Because you studied last night, you will know many answers on your math test this afternoon." My mother had slit open the cellophane wrapper, used tweezers to remove the original fortune, and then inserted her own message into the cookie. My fortune came true! I *did* know the answers because I had studied. She's always doing things like that. And yes, it does remind me that I get better grades when I study. By the way, my friends thought my mom was really cool for writing that fortune.

Praise is valuable when it points out specific behavior. So the next time your daughter is doing something right, take a moment and point out the positive behavior. Let her know you appreciate her efforts to practice the piano without your nagging. Acknowledge her attempt to fill the dog's water bowl on a hot day. It's all too easy to ignore children as they read a book in the car. But they certainly get our attention when you hear the familiar chorus of "Mom! Ashley's touching my elbow!"

Mother-Daughter Mini-Activity

The next time you have a day at home with your daughter, make sure you are each wearing pants with pockets. Ask your daughter to put 10 pennies in her right pocket and you do the same with your pocket. Throughout the day, whenever you make a negative comment to your daughter, such as "Emma, you're so lazy when it comes to your chores," she should quietly transfer a penny into her left pocket. Whenever you say something positive to your daughter, such as "That's a great birthday card you made for Grandma," slip a penny over to your left pocket. See who has all 10 of their pennies in the left pocket first. If your daughter announces her left pocket is full after 15 minutes, you'll know it's time to start looking for more positive communication techniques!

Brittany, an 11-year-old, told us: "Sometimes I really don't like to be home. My mom always gets on my case for everything. She tells me I'm a slob because of my messy room. She says my sister is smarter than me at math. She hates the way I wear my hair." Brittany's mom is probably telling the truth about Brittany's messy room and her math skills. But as adults, we need to find more appropriate ways to communicate our message. After all, weren't you tactful when a good friend bought a hideous dress and asked you, "Don't you just love this dress?"

Last week I reminded Sondra to empty the dishwasher, one of her assigned chores. After she left for school, I noticed that she had not only emptied the dishwasher but had also cleaned the kitchen counters, refilling the dishwasher with dirty dishes. I quickly left a voice mail message on her cell phone, thanking her for making the extra effort in cleaning the kitchen. It only took a few seconds, but let her know I appreciated what she did. The more we acknowledge our daughters' positive behavior, the more likely they are to continue acting in a responsible way. It's up to us to "catch" them doing well.

A San Francisco mom with two kids shares this idea of reinforcing positive behavior:

> "About twice a year, we take out a classified ad in the local paper, highlighting our children's positive accomplishments. The last ad read: 'Congratulations to Ericka Parker on an outstanding report card from Williamson Middle School. We're proud of you, Ericka!'"

Whether Ericka is embarrassed or not, she'll still feel good knowing her hard work at getting good grades is appreciated.

Sometimes we don't notice how easy it is to give negative comments to our daughters. Sondra and I just returned from playing tennis. It must have been mother-daughter day at the courts, because another mother and her 10-year-old daughter played next to us. The mom continually said, "Ariel, watch the ball.... You're so slow.... Come on, I'm not playing if you don't give it some effort.... Ariel, you missed that easy ball. Why should I play with you if you don't try? ... Don't be so slow." Ariel's face showed her discouragement. She lethargically hit the ball, avoiding eye contact with her mom.

Sondra noticed the negative comments, too. Naturally I had to get involved! In my best preschool teacher voice, I started giving enthusiastic play-by-play positive reinforcement to Sondra's moves. "Wow! Sondra, you sure followed through on that serve.... Great job! ... I can't believe how much you've improved! You are a great tennis player!" Sondra quickly caught on and began saying positive things about my pathetic playing. We really had a mutual admiration society going!

Within 10 minutes, the other mom picked up on our not-so-subtle cues. She began saying, "Ariel, that was a good hit. You really kept your eye on the ball." Within a few minutes, Ariel's attitude changed! She dashed after balls and served with flair. She even smiled at her mom. They walked off the courts chatting together in a totally upbeat mood. Ahhhh, the power of positive reinforcement.

Sondra says: I had a friend whose mother always nagged her. I don't think her mom meant to be mean, but she'd say things like, "Amy, you didn't pay attention when the coach was talking to you today. Your sister listens. Why can't you? Can't you do a better job cleaning your room?" I liked Amy. It was her mother that made me feel bad. Her mom would say those types of things, and then Amy would go in her room and tell me how much she hated her mom. I think you can tell your daughter she needs to clean her room in a more positive way.

Sometimes moms just need reassurance they are doing a good job dealing with a tween. (Just the fact you are reading this book makes you an above-average mom!) If you have a few minutes, look up www.parenting zone.com. This website offers tips on communicating with your tween, along with craft ideas and discipline techniques. All the information is presented in short articles and practical tips.

GUIDELINE #3: ENJOY YOUR DAUGHTER!

Robert Carlson became a best-selling author with his series of Don't Sweat the Small Stuff books. He encourages people to let go of trivial events and concentrate on seeing the overall picture. In *Don't Sweat the Small Stuff for Moms,* he reminds mothers that children don't care if you are a top-level executive. Children want mothers who take the time to listen, laugh, and be with them in a relaxed setting. Your daughter spills her milk? Get the dog to lick up most of it and then hand your daughter a sponge.

When Sondra was a preschooler, we often went mall-walking before the stores opened. She had free rein to run the length of the mall, waving to her senior citizen friends, who were strolling the mall for exercise. One day she decided to wear her tap shoes because they made such a delightful tap-tap sound as she walked the mall's tile floors. I met a friend who asked, "Why are you letting her wear tap shoes at the mall?" Why not? Sondra had a great time demonstrating her shuffle-ball-change-step to any person commenting on her tap shoes.

Today, I see Sondra as quite the individual, with little regard to "what others think." She's learned she gets positive feedback from being her own unique person. She's also learned that I enjoy being with her. (Well, most of the time!) It doesn't mean having to take your daughter out to a fancy dinner so you can have "quality time." One mom told me, "Sometimes when my daughter is in her room doing homework, I'll come in and read the paper lying on her bed. I tell her I just like being with her. Sometimes she continues doing her homework, and sometimes she'll use that opportunity to tell me about something bothering her."

When I appeared on the Fox reality show *Trading Spouses*, I spent a week with a family that had a few "relationship problems." I suggested that the dad take his tween daughter out for a fun activity so they could be together. He said, "I don't like being with her. She talks too much. She's hyperactive. Why would I want to spend time with her?" Even more horrifying is that his daughter was standing next to him as he said that. The little girl knew her dad didn't enjoy spending time with her. I'll never forget the dejected look on her face as she said, "Dad, it's okay. You don't have to go bowling with me if you don't want to." Fortunately, on the show, the contract states that he has to do whatever I ask. I told him (away from his daughter) that he had better take her bowling, turn off his stupid cell phone, and at least pretend to have a good time with her. I stressed how important it was for his daughter to know that her dad liked doing things together. A few hours later, she came home beaming at having spent time with her dad, and he sheepishly agreed it was a good idea to do something together.

An 11-year-old answering our survey wrote: "I think my mom just puts up with me. She buys me clothes. She drives me to my friends. But I think she thinks it's what she has to do. She hardly ever smiles at me." Another chapter in this book gives specific ideas for fun games and crafts you can do with your daughter. Beyond specific activities, find small ways to let your daughter know she is special to you. It's the small pat on the back or the invitation to go to pick up dry cleaning together that conveys you enjoy being with her.

Get more ideas on how to enjoy your daughter from www.familyeducation.com. The website lets you look up specific age-appropriate games and activities for you and your daughter.

Just for Fun

William Tell Target

Supplies needed: an apple and cotton balls

You probably have heard the story of William Tell. Because of a disagreement with the king, he was forced to shoot an apple off his son's head with an arrow. Don't worry; you're not going to use a bow and arrow on your daughter! Ask your daughter to stand against a wall and balance an apple on her head. Watch out! Apples are wobbly. When the apple is balanced, stand about five feet from her. Toss a cotton ball to try and hit the apple. How many tries does it take? Again, this is one of those activities that sounds boring on paper but elicits screams and cheers from your tween. Aren't you glad you're not using a bow and arrow? Now let your tween try to hit the apple on your head! (Don't let her bring out the bow and arrow either!) If you are brave, try tossing small foam balls or craft pom-poms. How about a small wet sponge?

Chapter 11

How Can We Have
Fun Together?

Just thinking about a mother's responsibility is exhausting. We try to instill self-confidence in our daughters, teach them to say "please" and "thank you," tell them we love them, worry they'll join a biker gang and tattoo their heads, provide homemade teddy bear cupcakes for the class parties, sew intricate costumes at Halloween, make multiplication flash cards, clean up middle-of-the-night vomit, teach them to write thank-you notes, and lose sleep worrying about upcoming college tuition. What about the *fun* of having a tween daughter? Let's not forget that our daughters are now potty trained and can tell us what they want without having a temper tantrum (most of the time). This chapter looks at the good times—the times when you and your daughter laugh together at a joke only the two of you understand.

Statistics show that a preschooler laughs an average of 400 times a day. (Those potty jokes are awfully funny!) Adults? They laugh a grand total of 15 times. Yes, it's important to have rules about bedtime and homework, but let's not forget the value in simply enjoying being together.

In surveying mothers across the country, we asked, "What's the best thing about having a tween daughter?" Here are some of their answers:

- "I have enjoyed sharing interests and all girl things. We laughed and giggled over things the males in the house just couldn't understand."
- "I get to experience that time in my life all over again and hopefully make it a fun time for both of us. I love spending time together and doing things we both love."
- "I love seeing her experience new things. My daughter is awesome! She talks to me and asks my advice. We have a wonderful mother-daughter relationship."

- "Sharing the fun girl stuff like shopping."

- "My 12-year-old daughter Leslie and I are very close. I love spending time with her, even just running errands, because she loves to talk and tell me everything. I love the energy and excitement of everyday that she exhibits. I love watching her do her hair, put her clothes together for the next day, all the while bebopping to her favorite music. It reminds me of my younger days."

- "There are more interests that we enjoy together."

- "We took a mother-daughter quilting class and had fun working on a quilt as a team. It's fun to talk and spend time with each other."

- "You won't be bored. Daily life is unpredictable. Each morning you never know if the day will be exciting, busy, dull, silly, memorable, dramatic, productive, wasted, satisfying, or exasperating. Put on your emotional seatbelt because it's gonna be a rocky ride!"

One of the best ways to enjoy that rocky ride is through the use of humor. Businesses frequently ask me to speak at conferences on how to reduce stress through the use of humor. Study after study shows that employees who have fun at work are more productive and take less stress-related sick days. Those same principles apply to your daughter. A fun-filled home atmosphere where people enjoy being around each other can only have a positive impact on your daughter.

This doesn't mean you need to put on a juggling show during breakfast and tell nonstop jokes. I remember when Trina was 12 and our community was socked in with a major ice- and snowstorm. Just before the power went out in our house, a radio station gave an urgent appeal for anyone with four-wheel drive to donate blankets to a nursing home that was without heat. The National Guard was bringing in generators, but they still wanted extra blankets for the residents. What else were we doing on this frigid night? We collected blankets and braved the treacherous roads, which were a solid sheet of ice. This is fun, you're asking? No, the fun comes after delivering the blankets. Even though it was 8:30 PM, as we drove home, Trina said, "Dad, I sure feel like a barbecued steak right now." "Great idea!" he responded, and pulled into a grocery store that was doing a brisk business in milk and bread, not so much in steaks labeled "Great for the BBQ." Half an hour later, the two of them stood outside in −2 degree weather, barbecuing steaks and singing campfire songs. I, on the other hand, curled up in bed with my St. Bernard snuggled next to me. Now, whenever there's a big snowstorm, Trina says, "Remember how much fun it was to barbecue during the blizzard?"

If you live in Florida, you'll obviously have to find other ways to have fun with your daughter than getting frostbite in a blizzard. In that case, try the Funny List.

In our house, we keep a valuable piece of paper in our fireproof strong-box. It's the Funny List. This document records events in our family that all three of us agree are of the highest forms of laughter or embarrassment. If you simply tell a funny story, that's not "Funny List worthy." However, if you are an 11-year-old named Sondra in a botanical garden, standing under a tree laden with papaya, singing a song about a papaya, and suddenly a papaya breaks loose and falls on your head—that gets on the Funny List. When you are the only male member of the Clark household and you're building a storage shed in the backyard and accidentally lock yourself inside and can only get out by removing an entire window, that makes the Funny List. (Granted, we have a unique sense of humor.)

It's a great honor to be on the Funny List. Allan will tell us something funny that happened to him at work and ask, "Did that make the Funny List?" The entire family (all three of us!) has to agree that the event deserves to be written down on the hallowed piece of paper and stored in the strongbox. If too much time goes by between entries, I offer a reward for someone who can do something to get on the list. Right now there's $50 for the next person who does something listworthy.

Last year, after a dry spell of funny incidents, I offered another $50 reward. A few weeks later, we took part in a mystery dinner train ride excursion. Different colorful characters passed through the train cars acting out segments of a play revolving around mixed identities and a murder. At the end, the hostess gave everyone paper and pencil to write his or her own ending to deduce the true murderer. I decided not to participate, but Sondra scribbled furiously on her entry. The hostess later appeared and said, "We have a first-place winner in our 'Who Murdered John McGillicutty' play. Would Silvana Clark please come up here so we can read her entry?" The win was quite a surprise, since I hadn't even entered. Sondra seemed to have an extra-large grin on her face, though. So there I stood, in front of all the passengers, as the hostess read what she thought was my entry. It sounded like a cheap romance novel with Patrick wanting to hold his body against Sophia's as she struggled in his arms trying to reach her true love, Sebastian. Let's not forget the descriptions of Sophia's body burning with passion and lust for the man wrongly murdered. It was a bad soap opera! Everyone laughed at my trashy writing, while Sondra held her hand out and kept mouthing, "Fifty dollars." Yes, she got her money and made the Funny List!

Mother-Daughter Mini-Activity

With your daughter, get some special paper with a fancy border or design at a craft store. Write "Funny List" on the top. Now, think back to a few funny experiences that have happened to your family and begin your list with those situations. Then start doing some funny things so you can continue to add events. Why not offer a monetary reward to kick-start this new family tradition?

The point of having fun is so your daughter enjoys being with you—even if she claims she's embarrassed to be seen in public with you. Sondra came home from school one day and said, "I don't know what you did, Mom, but all the kids at school think you and Dad are really cool." How's that for a compliment?

Ralph Waldo Emerson said, "Be silly, be honest, be kind." Most of us think about being honest and kind, but forget about being silly. Here are some ways to have fun with your daughter. Some ideas are simply things you can do to make her think you are fun (or that you've lost your mind). Other activities require her to participate. If she's reluctant, ask her to go along with your idea for 10 minutes. She'll usually get involved and forget about the time.

- Wake her up some morning dressed in an outlandish costume. Sprinkle sequins on her bed, which you call "Mom's Morning Wake-Up Powder."
- Get a book on making hand shadows. As she is lying in bed, impress her with your rabbit, turkey, and cow-getting-milked shadows on her wall.
- Make paper airplanes and see whose flies the farthest.
- Write words on her back with your fingers.
- Teach the dog a new trick together.
- Go on a "coin-flip" walk: As you walk out the front door, have her flip a coin. Heads means you turn right, tails turn left. See where you end up.
- See who can balance a broom on its end the longest. *Hint:* Look at the top of the broom as you balance it on the palm of your hand.
- Give your daughter an assortment of sponges and soft balls. Have her sit inside a room with a door that has space on both sides while you stand in the hall, out of view. The goal is for you to sprint across the open doorway like the mechanical ducks at a shooting gallery, as your daughter attempts to hit you with a foam ball. It's funnier than it sounds! (Be sure to add some quacking duck sounds!)
- Use watercolors to paint portraits of each other. Get the finished pictures professionally framed.
- Take a mother-daughter class together in quilting, hiking, or something that interests both of you.
- Perform the following easy magic trick that will amaze your daughter. Wear a short-sleeve shirt, and when she's not around, use clear lip balm to write her name on the inside of your forearm. Then stand in front of her and say, "I am the Amazing Mommeesta the Magnificent. I will now reveal the name of an amazing 11-year-old that I know." Sprinkle flour or colored sand over your arm, which looks completely normal, so your daughter won't suspect anything. Shake off the excess powder and her name will magically appear on your arm. Watch out, David Copperfield!

In my opinion, crafts are an ideal way for mothers and daughters to have fun together. It's not the finished project that counts, but the time spent together in a relaxed setting. I confess, Sondra began using a glue gun at age 4 to do craft projects. Now we both share the fact that our fingertips are permanently scarred from drops of hot glue. If you want a great resource for hundreds of craft ideas and supplies, check out S&S Worldwide (www.ssww.com). Its website and catalog offer complete craft kits, so you and your daughter can create projects ranging from jewelry to banners to woven baskets. It also offers craft kits ideal for groups of girls at birthday parties or sleepovers.

Below are some easy projects to try. Don't worry, nothing needs to meet Martha Stewart's standards. Feel free to adapt any ideas. Crafting is about fun, not perfection.

CD Sun Catchers

This is a fun way for moms and daughters to add some "sparkle" all through your house.

Gather these supplies:

2 old or unwanted CDs (for each sun catcher)

Assortment of inexpensive "puff paint" available at any craft store

Glue

Scraps of ribbon

Scissors

Follow these easy instructions:

1. Use the paint to draw designs on the unprinted sides of the two CDs.
2. Let dry.
3. Spread glue on the unpainted (label) side of one CD.
4. Cut a piece of ribbon about 12 inches long.
5. Make a loop with the ribbon, placing the two cut ends about an inch inside the CD with the glue.
6. Put the other CD on top, so that the painted sides are on the outside of your "CD sandwich."
7. Let the glue dry, then hang your decorated CD in a window to reflect the sun.

Flying Apple Butterfly Shirts

Moms and daughters could even use these shirts as matching nightgowns!

Gather these supplies:

Apples

1 solid-colored T-shirt that has been washed

An old magazine

Any color fabric paint

Paper plate for paint

2–3 contrasting colors of "puff paint"

Cutting knife

Follow these easy instructions:

1. Place your shirt on a flat surface such as a table or kitchen counter.
2. Slip the old magazine inside the shirt. This makes sure the paint doesn't soak through to the backside of the shirt.
3. Pour about 2 tablespoons of paint on the paper plate.
4. Cut the apple in half, starting from the top where the stem is. This creates a butterfly shape with the apple.
5. Press half the apple in the paint.
6. Press the paint-covered apple on the shirt. This is your butterfly image. Repeat the process, making as many butterflies as you want. You can make random prints or create a butterfly border around the neck of the shirt.
7. Let the paint dry overnight.
8. After paint is dry, use the puff paint to add embellishments. Add antennae or draw designs on the butterfly wings.
9. Let the puff paint dry and proudly wear your shirts!

Sondra says: Check to see if your craft store has glow-in-the-dark paint. Decorate your butterfly wings with this special paint that will shine when the lights are out!

"She Sells Seashells" Frame

Have you ever gone to the beach and collected buckets full of shells? Then you get home and wonder what to do with them! Here's a way to display your favorite shells and remind you of trips to the beach. (Of course, if you haven't collected shells, just put on your sunscreen and flip-flops and stroll to the craft store on a sunny day to buy a bag of assorted shells.)

Here's what you need:

Wooden frame, picture, or mirror (should be at least $1^1/_2$ inches wide so you have space to glue the shells)

Fine-grade sandpaper

Spray paint or acrylic paint in any color you want

Small paintbrush

Hot glue gun and glue sticks

String of inexpensive craft pearl beads (fake ones, not Grandma's antique pearl necklace)

Seashells! (Pretty obvious, isn't it?)

Just follow these easy steps:

1. Use the sandpaper to lightly sand the wooden frame. It works best to sand in the same direction as the wood grain.
2. Blow or brush off the minuscule wood particles on the frame.
3. Paint the frame. The color will barely show because of all the shells, but it gives a more complete look to the finished product.
4. Let the paint dry.
5. Use a hot glue gun and glue the string of beads around the frame opening. Decide if you want two or three rows of beads.
6. Pick four or five of your favorite shells and glue them in the corners or at the top of the frame.
7. Now simply continue using the hot glue to glue a few shells on at a time.
8. Continue until the entire frame is covered.
9. If you like, glue a few individual craft pearls in open spaces or even inside the shells.
10. If you decorated a picture frame, simply add your favorite photograph. If you decorated a mirror, polish the mirror and display your masterpiece!

Sondra says: If you and your daughter haven't used a glue gun before, start by using "low-temperature" glue pellets. It won't hurt as much when the glue gets on your fingers!

Bouquet of Beads

Sometimes you need a little accessory to go on a small shelf or table. These shiny bead bouquets will brighten up any area. Since they are so easy to make, display three or four in a colorful grouping.

Here's what you'll need:

Craft wire, around 26 gauge

Wire cutters (you can use old scissors or nail clippers to cut the wire also)

12mm Starflake beads

Smaller shiny beads, about 4mm (you can also use pearl beads)

Small vases with narrow necks

Follow these easy steps:

1. Cut sections of wire so they extend about 6–8 inches above your vase.
2. String a small bead over the end of the wire.
3. Bend the wire down so it overlaps about 2 inches.
4. From the bottom of the wire, string a Starflake bead so it is underneath the smaller bead.
5. You'll see a bit of wire underneath the Starflake bead. Twist it around the longer wire length to keep both beads secure. You've just made your first flower! Continue making various combinations of small beads and Starflake beads until you have all the flowers you need.
6. Place beaded flowers in your vase. Vary the stem length by bending the ends inside the vase.
7. Place your beaded flowers on a window and they'll really sparkle.

Sondra says: We made a bunch of these flowers and put them in a glass vase filled with leftover beads. It made them even more colorful.

Crafty Gumball Machine

Who doesn't like to put their money in a gumball machine, turn the creaky handle, and get a colorful piece of gum? Now you and your daughter can make a gumball machine that doesn't require a coin to get your treat!

Here's what you'll need:

6-inch flowerpot with drain tray

1 ivy bowl (available at any craft store)

1 2-inch wooden ball

Acrylic paint

Brushes

Precut foam shapes (optional)

Hot glue or craft glue

Gumballs!

Follow these easy steps:

1. Paint the wooden ball, flower pot, and drain tray a solid color.
2. Let the paint dry.

3. Use various colors to paint a design on your gumball machine. This is where you can get very creative.

4. If you want, attach precut foam shapes to decorate the machine.

5. Use a scrap piece of foam to write the price you are charging for the gum.

6. Assembly is easy. Simply turn flowerpot upside-down and glue bottom of ivy bowl to bottom of flowerpot.

7. Fill jar with gumballs or other candy.

8. Place flowerpot drain tray on top of ivy bowl.

9. Glue wooden ball on top of drain tray to serve as a handle.

Sondra says: Instead of filling my gumball machine with gum, I used it in my bedroom and kept my hair ties and clips in it. The ties are colorful and I just reach in and grab whatever I need when doing my hair.

Ready for some more ideas about the importance of having fun with your daughter? Do you ever automatically say no to your daughter when it's just as easy to say yes? I overheard a 10-year-old say to her mom after soccer practice, "Mom! It's a sunny day. Can we have a picnic in the backyard today?' Mom quickly answered, "Don't be silly. It's April. You only have picnics in the summer." Where's the law that says picnics only take place between June and August? How hard would it be to have a peanut butter sandwich in the backyard sitting on a blanket and enjoying the sunshine? If children are told no on a continuous basis, it's no wonder they get frustrated.

Instead of thinking about schedules and methods of discipline, think about adding an element of humor and spontaneity to everyday routines. Serve green eggs and ham for breakfast. Start a pillow fight. Try to laugh more than 15 times a day. Laughter unites a group in a positive, common experience. If you've just finished a game of hide-and-seek with your children, they certainly will be more receptive to your requests for help setting the table.

Sondra says: My mom and I are not always a perfect mother-daughter team. We have our fair share of arguments and disagreements. But my mom is right (yes, I actually said it) when she brings elements of fun into everyday activities. I am less likely to be resistant to something she tells me do when it's presented in a fun way. The mere fact that she went to the effort of making us eat dinner with tiny plastic play forks or set up a "pin the light on the Christmas tree" game, shows me she cares enough to give time and effort to creating fun. There's this overall lighthearted atmosphere that something fun is going to happen at our house. I might come home and find a giant green shamrock streamer around the border of my room for St. Patrick's Day or discover a funny quote on the steering wheel of my car.

A more relaxed style of parenting puts everyone in a better mood. Rather than nagging about books and dirty clothes in the rec room, put some of your favorite '60s and '70s rock 'n' roll music on and tell your daughter you'll keep playing it loudly until her things get put away. Now that's a threat that will get her moving!

One mom in Nashville with three daughters ages 10, 11, and 13 (whew!) told me:

> "I work full-time in a cafeteria, so the time with my daughters is precious. I plan some sort of fun activity with them every day. Sure, it's busy with different schedules, but I find a way to do something that is silly or just enjoyable. I actually write down the activity, like a menu. Last week on Tuesday we had a 'SPARKS' party. It only lasted about three minutes. The point is we did something together. [For all you potential party planners reading this book, a SPARKS party involves taking your daughter into a dark closet and simultaneously biting into a wintergreen Life-Saver. "Sparks" will fly out of your mouth.] On Thursday, we had a relaxed schedule, so after everyone had their pajamas on and was getting into bed, I yelled, 'Get in the car for ice cream!' We went one mile down the road and drove through the drive-up window at McDonald's."

Watching this woman interact with her daughters gave me that warm-and-fuzzy feeling. Their close relationship was so evident. She knew the importance of having fun together in the midst of homework, chores, and preadolescence.

One morning when Sondra was 12, she sat calmly eating breakfast before school. As the ever-dutiful mother, I was quizzing her on spelling words. Suddenly Allan burst through the door and yelled, "Sondra, I'm on my way to a meeting but I have exactly five minutes to challenge you to a game of tetherball!" She raced outside, barefoot and in pajamas, for a wild game of tetherball. Which do you think had a greater impact? Knowing that there are two *u*'s in the word *vacuum* or realizing that her dad thought enough of her to stop at the house on a workday morning?

That sense of joy and spontaneity helps children develop into an overall attitude of optimism about life. It's logical that the signs of a healthy family include the ability to foster a sense of humor among family members. One mother of two girls summed it up like this: "If I'm going to laugh about this situation in five years, why not just laugh about it now?"

That's all the fun for now. You have ideas for games, magic tricks, and crafts. Now get busy and do something worthy of an entry on the Funny List!

Just for Fun

Take your daughter to an antique store that sells knickknacks, embroidered aprons, and the like. Spend some time regaling her with tales of your first record player or metal Donny and Marie lunch box. When she's bored hearing about the "good old days," give her a predetermined amount of money. Have your daughter secretly pick you out a special teacup and buy it to use for mother-daughter tea parties. Then ask her to leave the area while you buy her a special teacup. Go home, exchange cups, and have some tea and crumpets.

Sondra says: We did this activity with our whole family. My mom, dad, and I drew names as to who would buy the other person's cup. (With just three of us, it wasn't much of a secret!) We went to a street of antique shops and each went into a different store to buy our teacups. When we got home, we wrapped them and had a little party giving the teacups to each other, and, of course, drinking tea. Whenever I see the cups in our china cabinet, I think about that fun family time together.

Chapter 12

The Joys of Tween Travel

Tired of the same mundane routine of school, Girl Scouts, and dance recitals? It's time to take a break and start traveling. Forget going to another mundane movie in your own community. Get your daughter out of the house to see new places and meet unique people! I can just hear you saying, "Wait! We don't have the money to take a cruise to the Mediterranean or jet over to Paris." No problem. Travel experiences await within 10 miles of your house.

I had a mother tell me she lived 12 miles away from a section of her town known as "Little Chinatown." She said (as I listened in amazement at her lost travel opportunity), "I've heard they have amazing authentic restaurants in Chinatown, along with outdoor stalls selling exotic herbs and spices. I'm scared to go there, though. What if we get lost?" I felt like yelling, "If you get lost, ask for directions!" Instead, I calmly encouraged her to make a Saturday afternoon adventure out of a mother-daughter excursion to Chinatown.

Your daughter will gain a wealth of cultural awareness by visiting ethnic communities in your area. It's eye-opening for a 12-year-old who is used to shopping at a sterile mall to walk down a narrow corridor in San Francisco's Chinatown and see tailors custom-fitting clothes. A Scandinavian community in the Seattle area sells lutefisk, a fish soaked in lye, which is considered a delicacy. Offer your daughter five dollars to take a bite!

Travel can mean driving an hour to a community Oktoberfest celebration. Watch the Shu-Plattler Dancers slap their leather pants and eat sauerkraut and sausage. The point is not to travel to Germany (although that's a wonderful experience!) but to experience another culture. For example, Lynden, Washington, a Dutch community complete with a giant windmill, sponsors Holland Days. The event starts with the traditional "washing of the streets." People dressed in traditional Dutch costumes, wearing wooden shoes, slather the streets with soapy water. As you attend these cultural events, ask your daughter to compare and contrast what she experiences with her own life.

Traveling through an Amish community gave our family a perfect tool for discussing why people would want to live without electricity, cell phones, and Starbucks. Sure, you could read a book about the Amish, but that can never take the place of stopping at an isolated farmhouse and having Sondra see a girl her age dressed in a homemade dress, milking a cow.

Just because you drive only a short distance from home doesn't mean you won't have a travel adventure. One holiday season we decided to visit a church that was sponsoring a "Walk-Through Bethlehem Experience." This free event invited the public to stroll through a re-creation of Bethlehem, complete with real camels, sheep, hundreds of biblically dressed characters, and even a live Baby Jesus. This church strove for authenticity—even in the parking lot, a "shepherd," complete with beard and long, flowing robe, greeted us. "Bethlehem is pretty crowded tonight," he said. "I'm going to have you be the first to park in the overflow parking lot. Follow this road up the hill and another shepherd will guide you to the remote parking area." We dutifully followed directions and met another costumed character who proceeded to give us more directions to the overflow lot.

Knowing that it's important to follow a shepherd's instructions, we headed off as directed. "Are you sure we weren't supposed to make a right turn?" asked Allan. I glibly assured him to continue driving. How hard is it to find a large parking lot? Soon the torch lights of Bethlehem were next to us. A sheep walked in front of the car, which we assumed was a stray from one of the pretend shepherds. Soon several other shepherds gave us quizzical looks. A few stray chickens, along with a family wearing flowing robes walked next to our car. Reality hit the three of us at the same time: "We're *driving* through Bethlehem!" Our modern-day Ford Contour was driving down Main Street Bethlehem, carefully avoiding animals, costumed characters, and the general public.

"Back up! We haven't gone that far!" I yelled. With clenched teeth, Allan said, "I can't back up. There are two camels walking behind me." I advised him to quickly turn left. His response, once more with clenched teeth, was, "If I turn left, I will run over Baby Jesus, sleeping in the manger." Turning right would have resulted in damage to the "Bethlehem Bakery" tent. We had no choice but to slowly drive down the main street of Bethlehem for a quarter of a mile. Normally that's a short distance. But when you're trying to avoid both chickens and a crowd of people, it seemed like a cross-country road trip.

See? You can have unique travel experiences in your very own community!

Sondra says: My mom and I took a weekend trip to a rural area of Indiana. We went to the town of Santa Claus and visited Holiday World (www.holidayworld. com), a first-class amusement park and water park without the commercialism of Disneyland. Then we spent the night at the Lake Rudolph campground. (Get it? Lake Rudolph in the town of Santa Claus?) Rather than sleeping in a tent, we rented an RV, complete with TV and refrigerator. Instead of going to a commercial museum like Ripley's Believe It or Not!, we went to a museum owned by a man that loves collecting antique musical instruments, including giant Dutch street organs. Yes, we visited Dr. Ted's Musical Marvels! Of course, since we were in Santa Claus, Indiana, we ate at St. Nick's restaurant.

That evening, we drove to one of the few drive-in theaters left in the country. It was so weird to drive our car onto this grassy field and attach speakers to hear the movie. Then my mother had to tell me stories of all the "wild" things she and her friends did at drive-ins! I've never even been to a drive-in with friends because there aren't any in our town.

Look at travel as an opportunity to expose your daughter to a world of possibilities. She'll see that people make a living training animals at Sea-World. Your daughter will learn that some people eat rice and beans for breakfast, if you drive just across the border to Tijuana, Mexico. She'll see history come to life by visiting a living history museum.

We visited Connor Prairie History Museum when Sondra was 12. During a demonstration of butter making, the museum docent selected Sondra to help churn butter. Sondra willingly raised the butter churn over and over as the docent explained the process. And explained it some more. And some more ... Fifteen minutes later, the lecture continued as Sondra kept churning the butter. We could see her arms get tired, but it was such a joy to see her do physical labor! After 20 minutes of churning, the docent motioned Sondra to stop so everyone could sample her churned butter. For the next few days, Sondra reminded us how hard she worked to provide that tiny dollop of butter we tasted. Her travel experience taught her a practical history lesson about pioneer life.

As you go on vacation, find ways to experience something besides the typical tourist activities. Many books and articles, with titles such as "Hidden Attractions in Florida" or "Off the Beaten Path in San Diego," provide ideas to enhance your travel adventures. We visit New York on a regular basis and had seen the Empire State Building, Ellis Island, the Statue of Liberty, and so forth. On our last visit, instead of revisiting the traditional attractions, we signed up for a bike tour through Harlem! Sunday morning found us pedaling through Harlem to experience a side of New York most tourists never see.

A new trend in family vacations is incorporating volunteer work with fun and games. Of course, you do all the typical vacation events such as swimming, relaxing, and wild roller coaster rides. A few days of the trip, however, are spent volunteering.

> *Linda, a mom and schoolteacher:* "We were taking a cruise that left from New Orleans. We left two days early so our family could help clean up damage from Hurricane Katrina. Our cruise was more meaningful because we saw how lucky we were to have a home undamaged by wind and floods."

It's all too easy for families to get in a rut of eating at the same pizza place, watching the same TV shows, and communicating in the same style. Travel gets you out of your rut! Have your daughter look through the brochures at the hotel and select a family activity. Encourage her to ask the concierge for suggestions on a unique restaurant. Offer a prize to a family member that can spell *concierge*. Often families discover that communication improves as family members find themselves in the situation of being in a new environment together. Work with your daughter on selecting a rental car. Ask her opinion about which museum to visit. She'll gain skills that transfer over to everyday life.

Travel also provides the opportunity for just plain mother-daughter fun. Kyle McCarthy, editor of a wonderful travel newsletter, says:

The tween years are the perfect time for girls to be introduced to the indulgences of travel by their mothers. Whereas you might not treat your child to a gourmet meal or a fancy pedicure as part of your home routine, many family resorts and cruise ships are making it easy and affordable to do so on vacation. Mother/ Daughter spa treatments, beauty applications ranging from skin care to glamour looks, family yoga classes, and many fine dining opportunities are available.

Get more tips on family travel from www.familytravelforum.com.

So, the next time you travel, you can spend the first day removing rubbish from a hurricane-damaged home and enjoy the next day getting a manicure with your daughter!

No matter what your budget, try to find ways to travel with your daughter. We spent a great three weeks traveling through Europe and staying in hostels the entire time. We'd find Sondra chatting with travelers from around the world, sharing experiences together. One night she joined a group of school kids from Austria in a talent show. The hostels provided clean, inexpensive rooms, along with the chance to meet people from various countries.

Experiences like that gave Sondra the confidence to start a conversation with anyone in any situation. Here's her experience at a camp in Spain, as she taught English to Spanish teenagers.

Sondra says: Summer camp is an American institution. Arts and crafts, swimming, ridiculous skits, and Crazy Olympic team activities are a part of most kids' summers. Take all those standard activities, mix in teens from English-speaking countries with native Spanish teens, and you have the recipe for the English Town teen program sponsored by Vaughan Village. English Town is a full-immersion English-language camp for Spanish teens. Most of the Spaniards who attend have had English in school and can read English well. However, when it comes to understanding, "Wow, he's pretty hott," or "You're really dragging this morning," the Spaniards respond with confused looks.

English Town recruits Anglos (English-speaking teens) to come and spend a week simply talking with the Spaniards. The Anglos need only to pay their round-trip ticket to Madrid. All meals, lodging, and other expenses are paid for by Vaughan Village. This means teens from the United States, Ireland, Canada, South Africa, Australia, and Great Britain get to enjoy a free week at camp in Spain.

I got the opportunity to spend a week in La Alberca, Spain, participating in the program. The city of La Alberca is straight out of the movies, a picturesque 18th-century village complete with cobblestone streets, overflowing flower baskets, street vendors, a fountain in the middle of the city courtyard, and the occasional donkey roaming the ancient streets. Like the city, our cabins had Old World charm, without the Old World amenities. Each Anglo shared a room with a Spaniard to encourage constant English conversation. Our room was so new, it still had paint smell coming from the walls. It was equivalent to any modern four-star hotel in the United States.

We were awakened in the mornings in typical camp fashion with counselors yelling in megaphones, blowing whistles, and blaring music. As we all came to the meeting room for breakfast, Anglos and Spaniards chatted about everything from their lives at home to American pop music. Every day, we were assigned a Spaniard to spend an hour talking one-on-one. The first day, the Spaniards were terrified and self-conscious about their English. The Anglos were worried they wouldn't have enough to talk about and would have to resort to awkward staring. All fears were settled when we sat down and started chatting about our families, schools, and friends. Conversation flowed freely. Many of the Spaniards I talked to knew more about the U.S. government then I did! I got into lively debates about world issues and politics. The mix of teens made it a wonderful experience. We swam, played volleyball, sang songs, and of course, went shopping together.

At the end of the week, there is a mad dash to collect everyone's e-mail addresses. I still converse with many of the other teens I met in Spain and have made wonderful friendships that will continue.

Vaughan Village offers four summer sessions that teens can attend. Although it was a wonderful and fun experience, talking slowly for a week and having to decipher what everyone is trying to say through all the world accents can be tiring. It's worth it, though, to see the improvements my new Spanish friends made as they went home, knowing more English than can be taught from a book. In addition to the teen program, there is also an adult program that runs year-round. My parents attended that program while I went to the teen camp. We were about six hours apart, so parents can't come and check up on their teens (which is a good thing for the teens☺). To find out more information about the program and to apply, the website is www.vaughanvillage.com.

What Sondra didn't tell you about is her cookie-making experience. While talking with the Spanish teens about food, she saw that many of them didn't understand "cookies." "Let's bake cookies!" she suggested. Sondra led the group into the camp kitchen and began making cookies (without a recipe). After the batter was mixed, she showed them the all-American tradition of eating raw cookie dough. The batter soon disappeared, and those Spanish teens never got a chance to eat baked cookies!

I figure if Sondra can handle a week at camp in Spain, she can handle an admissions interview for college! Travel has given her a global perspective as well as practical skills in safety, communication, and a desire for adventure.

Karen, a systems analyst, came up to me after a parenting workshop and said, "I'm sad at how we spent our family vacations. Ever since our daughters were 8 and 10, we'd spend two weeks at the same condo in Hawaii. Basically all we did was lay by the pool and go out to dinner. I see now how I wasted an opportunity to explore Hawaii with my daughters." It's not too late to foster a positive attitude toward travel!

Again, as a mom, it's up to you to expose your daughter to the delights and pitfalls of travel. Yes, planes get delayed and cars get stuck in traffic jams. We once had a 12-hour layover at Heathrow Airport . . . on Christmas Day! The airport was deserted and even the usual gift shops had "Closed" signs on the door. We walked outside and found some back roads to explore that would not have been possible if we were racing to a connecting flight.

Another time, Sondra and I were walking in a small town in Peru. I'd filled my backpack with baby clothes, intending to give them to some of the many women begging by the side of the road. Coming down a deserted alley, we saw a pregnant woman with a toddler, leaning against a stone wall. Opening my backpack, I handed her a few pieces of clothing. As if by magic, about 20 other women appeared, all trying to grab clothing and chattering at me in Spanish. They pushed and shoved trying to get close to my backpack, which also held our passports. Sondra kept yelling, "Let's go, Mom!" But with my back against the wall and women pressing against me, I couldn't move. Sondra, standing slightly outside the crowd, grabbed my wrist and jerked me away. We ran down the alley, dropping baby clothes along the way. That's one way to get the adrenaline going!

As your daughter participates in lessons about diversity in school, she'll have an awareness of what that means from her travel experiences. If you live in a middle-class, primarily Caucasian neighborhood, riding a New York subway is a true lesson in diversity! Think what your daughter learns from sitting next to people of various races. She hears foreign languages, sees different clothing styles, and learns that you better move fast before those subway doors close!

When Sondra was five, we were riding a bus through Vancouver, British Columbia, which is known for its diverse population. A man with a turban sat in front of us. Naturally, Sondra noticed a turban wasn't typical headgear. She tapped him on the shoulder and politely asked, "Excuse me. What's that on your head?" (I admit, I was a little embarrassed at her boldness.) He laughed and gave her a detailed explanation, much to the delight of people sitting around us.

All these travel experiences, pleasant or slightly unpleasant, give your daughter a global perspective. She understands that "her way is not the only way." When we moved to Nashville from Seattle, restaurants served us grits. Grits? It's easy to say, "How can I eat that tasteless white goopy stuff?" However, traveling has given our family the adventurous spirit of trying different foods. Now we drink sweet tea and get coleslaw *inside* our barbecue sandwich. I did draw the line at eating guinea pig in Peru, though. Restaurants serve whole, roasted guinea pigs as a meat entrée. Allan tried one and said, "It tastes like chicken with tiny, tiny bones!" Strange foods aside, taking your daughter to a nearby community for an ethnic festival or traveling overseas will provide her with experiences unavailable from a book or TV.

> Kim Orlando, *author of another travel website, www.travelingmom. com:* "It is the experience of a trip that I treasure and think that my daughter will remember. Like taking surfing lessons in California and having the opportunity to learn something new, together. An important part of that education was for her to see her mom fail and get up and try again ... and again. It's not only important to me that my daughter see the world but to take part in it—wherever she is. Anytime a young person travels away from home, it is a chance to see themselves in a different context—a smaller fish in an expanding pond. It offers a sense of possibility."

When asked on a survey what she would like to change about her life, 12-year-old Monica said: "I never do anything fun. I just stay home and watch TV with my brother. I wish I could do something exciting." Travel provides an incredible opportunity to give your daughter new experiences.

Again, you don't need a Donald Trump budget to see the world beyond your community. We recently traveled one hour from our house to the "Thrift Store Capital of the World." The tiny town claimed to have more thrift stores than any other city. We poked around in various dusty shops, many owned by grizzled men spitting tobacco on the floor. It truly felt like we had entered another world, far from the sterile world of a Gap at the mall. Many museums offer free admission on certain days of the month.

We have no qualms about saving \$15–25 by visiting a museum on Thursday night rather than Saturday morning.

Mother-Daughter Mini-Activity

Check out the travel section of your local Sunday newspaper. Most papers offer travel suggestions within easy driving distance. Have your daughter select a destination or event for the two of you to attend. You might find yourself experiencing a Renaissance Faire or visiting an onion festival where you sample onion ice cream!

If you're going on a simple weekend travel extravaganza, incorporate new experiences into your adventure. When stopping for ice cream, encourage your daughter to try a new flavor. If your family is sports oriented, change the focus and visit an art museum. Our family loves musicals, so we're very comfortable with theater "etiquette," whether on Broadway or at a local theater production. For a new experience, we decided to attend a professional football game. We soon discovered that football fans are quite different from the theater crowd! Still, we found ourselves cheering for the home team Seattle Seahawks and simply ignored the swearing from people around us when a pass got intercepted. I also learned that football games don't have an "intermission"—it's called "halftime"!

As you can tell, travel plays a big part in the Clark family. One of our biggest adventures involved a full year of family travel adventures. In August 2002 we decided to rent out our house and travel around the country in an RV for a year. The skeptics were amazingly vocal in telling us why a 12-month trip around the U.S. in an RV was foolish and open to disaster. "Don't you think this family togetherness is going too far?" "Why would you want to spend a year in such close proximity to your husband and preteen daughter?" "You'll drive each other crazy!" We were even more vocal in defending our position that togetherness on the road would only strengthen our family.

Naive thinking you ask? We reeked of naiveté when it came to RVing. As a professional speaker, I'm used to staying in luxury hotels with chocolate-covered strawberries waiting for me. (At the Quinault Resort and Casino, I actually had chocolate *and* gold-leafed strawberries waiting for me in my room.) We weren't exactly a poster family for roughing it in a campground.

The trip involved more than just fun. Sondra, 12 at that time, is a spokesperson for Childcare Worldwide, a faith-based relief agency. She's traveled to Africa and Peru to see its programs and frequently speaks at churches and schools, asking people to sponsor a child in a Third World country. She had a positive response from groups in our community, so we decided to "hit the road" and have her speak at a different church every Sunday as we traveled around the United States. In between the Sundays was time to relax and see the sights. My husband took a leave of absence from work, and we home-schooled Sondra. With my job, I simply flew to my speaking engagements from whatever airport we were closest to.

Without even a weekend camping trip under our belt, we headed off to the world of full-time RVing. My husband was a school bus driver trainer, so driving our rig was not a problem. (Really cool, in-the-know people call their RVs "rigs.") We could easily get from place to place. Figuring out what to do upon arrival at the campground was the time creative thinking began. "What's the difference between gray water and black water?" my husband asked a fellow camper the first night at an RV park. The large sign posted the message "Empty Gray Water First!" Our introduction to RV camping began with a graphic description that gray water comes from the gray tank that held sink and shower drainage. The black water comes from the black tank that held toilet waste. Important information to know. We'll also leave it to your imagination about what happens when the hose from the black tank breaks loose and sprays you with the foul-smelling substance.

Within a few days, the mechanics of driving, setting up at the campground, and hooking up to cable TV seemed as easy as normal household chores. The "fifth wheel" RV had a full-size refrigerator, microwave, stove, and TV. What more could we want? Allan's the chef in the family, so he continued making delicious meals, which we usually ate outside at our campsite. Sondra frequently did schoolwork outside also. On Sundays, we'd put on "good clothes" and give a presentation at a local church. An added bonus was meeting people at church and being invited to their homes for meals. We soon tasted regional specialties such as chili served over noodles and sandwiches spread with coleslaw. Sunday evenings we'd be back in our fifth wheel, ready to set off for another adventure in a different community.

That's when we discovered ... we liked being together! Each evening, after spending the day within close proximity of each other, Sondra would cuddle with us in bed, reading or writing in her diary. It seemed the more we were together, the closer we felt. My husband Allan and I took long, hand-holding walks in the morning while Sondra snoozed.

Every few days found us in a new location with opportunities to explore—even if it just meant finding the closest Wal-Mart. We set our own schedules. Feel like a midafternoon nap? No problem. Want to ride bikes before breakfast? Get your helmet and head out. This will sound like a sound bite from Dr. Phil, but we really did discover the joy of quality and quantity family time. I wish I could confess to dramatic arguments and a need to "have my own space," but other than a few minutes of tension here and there, our trip contained few negative experiences.

I was under contract to write a book and doing research on the internet was difficult. So, I'd go to local libraries, asking for a guest pass to use their computer. Often I was allowed only 30 minutes of computer use. Frustrated, I'd come home, complaining how I'd never get my book finished if I couldn't use a computer. It worked out, though, and my book was completed ahead of deadline.

Overall, I'd attribute the success of our trip to the fact that we are all pretty flexible. We adapt to change and don't have to do things a certain way. As far as positive experiences, well, here are just a few:

- Arriving in Sturgis, South Dakota, during the largest rally of motorcycles in the world and meeting incredibly polite Harley-Davidson guys. (Did they really have to call me "Ma'am"?)
- Racing to the store on October 31 in Peru, Indiana, so we'd have candy as kids went rig to decorated rig in the RV campground yelling "Trick or treat!"
- Visiting the corporate headquarters of Lands' End, in Dodgeville, Wisconsin, and seeing their incredible swimming pool and employee fitness center.
- Staying in a hotel designed by Frank Lloyd Wright in Wisconsin and unknowingly racking up a $143 bill for using the internet.
- Visiting a small church in Nashua, New Hampshire, where the majority of people attended that Sunday because they got a free Thanksgiving turkey. We ended up eating our Thanksgiving dinner at Plymouth Rock in Massachusetts, where the pilgrims landed in 1620.
- Spending Christmas at a campground in Hershey, Pennsylvania, where the air smelled like chocolate. Hershey is one of the largest manufacturers of chocolate products, so we enjoyed their free samples!
- Using our hair dryer to unfreeze water pipes to our rig in Haskell, Tennessee. (Did I mention that only really cool people call their RV a "rig"? We later learned that really cool people also spend January in Florida with their rigs.)
- Attending an all-African-American church in Chattanooga, Tennessee, in honor of Martin Luther King Jr. Day.
- Driving through Amish country in Lancaster, Pennsylvania, on a Sunday evening as families walked or drove their buggies home from Sunday services.
- Making a detour to the Grand Canyon for a nine-day river-rafting trip.
- Home-schooling (or should I say RV-schooling?) Sondra by visiting museums, historic landmarks, birthplaces of presidents, plantations, factories, festivals, and monuments. How could a textbook ever compare to visiting Helen Keller's birthplace in Tuscumbia, Alabama, and learning how she overcame being deaf and blind?
- And, of course, Wall Drugs in South Dakota. This touristy drugstore has signs around the world saying "Visit Wall Drugs!!!" In Seoul, Korea, the signs say: "Wall Drugs, 6,636 miles." In Amsterdam, the sign informs you that Wall Drugs is only 5,387 miles away. Naturally, we stopped to see the store, filled with an assortment of rattlesnake ashtrays, western art, and buffalo burgers.

It's been four years since we returned to living in a house that remains in the same place day after day after monotonous day. I still get a lump in my throat seeing a fifth wheel RV cruise merrily down the road, off to a new discovery. The emotional effects of the 25,000-mile trip are long lasting. Sondra, now 17, doesn't mind hanging out with her two middle-aged parents. And yes, she still cuddles with us in bed while reading or writing in her journal. For now, Allan and I, like most mature adults, face the reality of jobs and bills. On a daily basis, though, we talk about our 25,000 miles of memories and plan our next on-the-road adventure. This time, however, we'll head out as experts on the intricacies of black water tanks.

I know not everyone can take a year off to travel around the country. Wait a minute! If our family did it, why can't you? The point is, travel is crucial to helping your daughter develop a tolerance for various cultures and lifestyles while developing a global awareness. If you can't travel, find ways to bring distant places to you. Get a cookbook and make French crepes or Italian gelato. Learn a few words of another language. Have a foreign-exchange student spend a few weeks with your family. Rent some of Rick Steves's travel videos that provide low-cost and informative travel experiences.

Sondra says: I love to travel. When we moved to a new house, I asked for a room-sized map of the world. It came in three sections, like big pieces of wallpaper. Now my 10-foot by 12-foot wall is completely covered with a map of the Earth. I love laying in bed and looking at all the places I want to discover.

If you like armchair travel, consider looking at some of these websites to get more ideas:

- www.hamptoninnlandmarks.com. Hampton Inns offer clean, affordable family accommodations across the country. Be sure to check out this website, where they describe unique places to visit such as a 20-foot duck in Flanders, New York, and a 42-foot statue of Uncle Sam in California. Mom, you might want to head to St. Augustine, Florida, to drink water from the Fountain of Youth!
- www. firestone.com. Look at "Legendary Drives" on this website to find descriptions of great road trips across the country. Just click on your state and see where you can go this weekend! They also ask for submissions of scenic travel photos. Encourage your daughter to take a travel picture and submit it to their website.
- www.roadsideamerica.com has listings of offbeat tourist attractions, such as the world's largest cherry pie pans and bridges built so frogs can safely cross busy streets.
- www.childrenmuseum.com provides information on—you guessed it—children's museums around the country.
- www.travelingmom.com
- www.familytraveltimes.com

- www.familytravelforum.com
- www.travelwithkids.com

However, nothing beats actually seeing some of the fascinating sights around the country and around the world. Some great destinations are listed below.

The Lucerne Hotel in New York City (www.thelucernehotel.com), located near the Museum of Natural History, was once a college dorm. The rooms have been enlarged, though! Staff are friendly to children, and minifridges are in each room. Our family brings plastic bowls and cereal with us when we travel to New York. That way, we pick up some milk at a local deli and we're all set for breakfast.

Loews Hotels offer a "Loews Loves Kids" program designed to make kids feel extra special. (They also offer a "Loews Loves Pets" program for those pampered four-footed family members.) The Coronado Bay Resort on Coronado Island in San Diego (http://loewshotels.com/en/hotels/coronado bay-resort/) is an ideal location for family fun. The flat island lends itself to plenty of beach access as well as level bike trails. Supervised kids pro grams from toddlers to teens provide scavenger hunts, surfing lessons, games, and crafts. Then just drive across the Coronado Bridge and you're almost at the San Diego Zoo and SeaWorld.

Does your tween enjoy being around animals? Check out some animal-related activities.

Larson's Famous Clydesdales. The tiny town of Ripon is home to Wisconsin's top agriculture-related tourist attraction. For 27 years, Judy and her husband Cal have owned and trained Clydesdales to use in hitching competitions. Six days a week, this horse-happy couple opens their home for a fast-paced, 90-minute tour and show.

Judy is up at 4:00 AM to give her horses baths. Of course, there are horses to feed, saddles to polish, and 400 bags of popcorn to fill. She personally answers the phone to take tour reservations. And let's not forget the "super-size" task of cleaning horse stalls! During the season (May to October), up to 400 people a day arrive for tours of the barns, museum, and the two 40-foot trailers pulled by custom-built trucks. Then it's showtime!

Judy and Cal have set up a show yard, complete with covered bleachers. Judy's running commentary about their success as Clydesdale-owning, hitch-driving competitors is interspersed with tricks from two live-wire dogs and jokes about Cal. Cal, dressed in formal "attire," accepts the kidding and proceeds to give a fascinating performance with his horse.

The tour at Larson's Famous Clydesdales gives an oasis of genuineness only one hour from tourist-friendly Wisconsin Dells. Your daughter will get a rare glimpse into the lives of a couple who make a living following their passion. *Larson's Famous Clydesdales, W12654 Reeds Corner Road, Ripon WI 54971, www.larsonsclydesdales.com, 920-748-5466*

Regenstein Center for African Apes. If your opinion is that "all zoos are alike," then head over to the Lincoln Park Zoo in Chicago (open 365 days a year with free admission) and visit the new Regenstein Center for African Apes. This $26 million facility is a state-of-the-art interactive facility for the zoo's 24 apes. Yes, *interactive.* At first glance, the facility looks like a modern-day ape enclosure, complete with waterfall, vines, trees, and mulch-covered floors. However, hidden from visitors' view is the ape version of a surprise attack from a Super Soaker. Chimps can touch a panel that shoots harmless blasts of air at unsuspecting visitors. Steve Ross, a behaviorist at the zoo, says the air blasts help chimps interact with visitors. Instead of apes banging on glass to get screams of surprise from visitors, the air blasts produce the same end result.

The new exhibit has bells and whistles (literally) for apes to use. Ape-controlled fans let the furry creatures cool themselves when Chicago's humidity rises. And for even more action, hungry apes can touch panels in fake tree trunks that catapult snacks through the air. Yes, going to the zoo to see rare birds, lions, and penguins is a delightful way to spend the afternoon. But for a new experience, try watching apes toss snacks through the sky and blast you with air! *Lincoln Park Zoo, 3001 N. Clark Street, Chicago IL 60614, www.lpzoo.com, 312-742-2000*

Oregon Trail Wagon Train. Does your daughter consider it a hardship when her laptop computer needs to be recharged? Perhaps a few days spent reliving the experiences of our pioneer forefathers would put "hardship" in perspective. The Oregon Trail Wagon Train tours offer a chance to get dusty, thirsty, and jostled around in a covered wagon. Don't worry, it's not all dirt and work, there's plenty of time for fun.

Modern-day pioneer families can choose from an overnight trek or a four-day version. The main animal contact will be with the horses pulling the wagons. On the trail, children help groom and feed the horses. They even get the chance to control the horses while driving the wagon. The horses become an integral part of the "team" in getting the wagon from place to place.

This tour is ideal for families with daughters fascinated with *Little House on the Prairie.* Children also earn the value of animals. At the end of the day, horses receive their water and "dinner" before people. This wagon trail trip will open your daughter's eyes to a world where people and animals work together toward a common goal. *Oregon Trail Wagon Train, Bayard NE 69334, www.oregontrailwagontrain.com, 308-586-1850*

For some people, taking an organized tour is a great experience. Let someone else worry about meals, bus connections, and museum hours!

Order the Backroads catalog (www.backroads.com) for hours of armchair travel possibilities. Don't stop at just looking at the pictures, though. Sign up for a wide selection of around-the-world travel opportunities. You can experience multisports adventures in Europe or hiking and biking trips in the U.S. Each trip includes a trained kid's coordinator, so adults get fun also!

Want something a little more exotic? Check out Thompson Family Adventures (www.familyadventures.com) if you think a trip to Belize, China, Peru, or Tanzania would appeal to your family. You'll have a deluxe tour, and your daughter will get matched up with an overseas pen pal to develop a cross-cultural relationship. Thompson Family Adventures schedules tours around school vacations and provides free travel insurance.

Feeling slightly more adventurous but still want some structure to your vacation? Check out one of these all-inclusive resorts:

- Costa Rica is becoming a popular tourist destination. Banana Bank Lodge in Costa Rica (www.bananabank.com) offers jungle equestrian adventures, along with boating and tubing tours. Your daughter will enjoy seeing the animal rehabilitation center on the property.

- Then there's the Jaguar Reef in Belize (www.jaguarreef.com). It offers a "Walk on the Wild Side" program that includes lodging, meals, and adventure trips to surrounding locations. How does floating on an inner tube through a cave sound? Jaguar Reef sits on a 600-acre peninsula and offers amazing snorkeling. Stay in cabanas or suites to continue that mother-daughter bonding experience!

- If you like the Caribbean, Wyndham Resorts (www.wyndamresorts.com) offers all-inclusive packages that let you enjoy meals, tween programs, water sports, and luxury accommodations. Your daughter will meet friends her own age while participating in water carnivals and disco dances.

- Think how you would impress your friends if you said, "We're going to the Turks and Caicos." (Where is that?) Actually, the Turks and Caicos Islands are halfway between Florida and Puerto Rico. Beaches Resorts (www.beaches.com) offers several all-inclusive locations for carefree fun on one of the largest reefs in the world. Again, meals, accommodations, and most activities are included in one flat price. Relax in the spa, snorkel, swim in the ocean or pool, and send your daughter off to the tween program.

I admit I'm biased about the joy of riding bikes through Europe. After all, it was on a bike ride in Holland that Allan and I decided to get married, over 31 years ago. We even led a month-long bike tour for 21 people through Europe in 1983. Now, I encourage you to get on a bike and take a tour through www.biketoursdirect.com. They'll help you find the ideal route for you and your daughter, ranging from a leisurely ride along the Danube River to a route between Florence and Rome. Select a guided tour, and you'll travel with tour guides helping you with luggage transfers, hotel reservations, sightseeing expeditions, and meals. Feeling more independent? Go the self-guided route. You'll still have hotel reservations confirmed. All you do is follow the maps to get from place to place. Either way, you'll see a part of Europe you'd never experience from a large tour bus. Plus, all the exercise of riding bikes counteracts the calories from all the delicious pastries you'll consume stopping at authentic bakeries.

The popularity of cruises provides you with travel opportunities for every budget. We've taken a low-cost five-day Carnival cruise to Cozumel, Mexico, that is ideal for first-time cruisers. You don't have to worry about getting your luggage to the room or where to eat. Kids have organized activity programs. Our favorite cruise, though, was an Alaskan cruise on Holland America (www.hollandamerica.com). The ship was certainly family friendly, but we weren't overrun with kids. The staff quickly learned Sondra's name and remembered her favorite flavor of ice cream. Allan and I enjoyed the speakers and naturalists on board, while Sondra rehearsed for a stage presentation. If you're looking for a cruise that caters to more than families with children, check them out. They even offer cruises to Africa!

Looking for something closer to home? Jekyll Island Club Hotel (www.jeykllisland.com) is located ... on an island! Enjoy special family vacation packages that include supervised children's activities and a first-class playground. In addition, families can explore 10 miles of beach, ride horses, and visit the Georgia Sea Turtle Center. Twenty miles of paved trails lets the family enjoy safe bike riding. Canoes and kayaks are available to explore the inland waterways. No chance of being bored!

Like the outdoors? The Snowbird Ski and Summer Resort (www.snowbird.com) has it all, year-round. In the winter, kids under six ski free. You can also enjoy snowmobiling, tubing, and snowshoeing. Summer activities include a 1,000-foot zip line, an alpine slide, aerial trams, and musical events.

If you're still hesitant about spending a week outside the comfort of your usual vacation destination, then try a one-day trip. Get your daughter and try a single-day adventure such as river rafting or hang gliding—yes, hang gliding! We recently spent an exhilarating morning floating at 2,000 feet above the ground near Chattanooga, Tennessee. Lookout Mountain Flight Park (www.hanglide.com) is the largest full-time hang gliding school and resort in the United States. Even its overnight cabins are shaped like hang gliders! You'll fly with a certified instructor (who, I hear, still has a headache from having me scream in his ear while we flew). An ultralight plane tows you and your instructor up and up and up ... until at 2,000 feet, the tow line is released and you get 12 to 20 minutes to silently glide through the air. It's an experience that will give you and your daughter hours of conversation.

Just for Fun

Get hold of two books that will certainly whet your appetite for traveling. *1001 Places to See before You Die* by Patricia Schultz describes—get ready—1,001 places you should see before you die! I've begun giving this book as a wedding present to young couples, encouraging them to travel rather than buying an expensive leather couch. Then there's *500 Places to Take Your Kids before They Grow Up* by Holly Hughes. This 576-page book will inspire you to forget about armchair traveling and hit the road. Your tween daughter will soon be a teenager with summer jobs, a boyfriend (yikes!), and plans of her own. Quick! Before it's too late, grab your tween daughter and start traveling!

Chapter 13

Three Things Your Daughter Needs to Know (According to Silvana)

Look through any parenting book and you'll find that experts tell you girls need to know how to read, pay attention in school, be respectful, wash their hands after using the bathroom, color inside the lines, wait their turn, and put dirty clothes in the hamper. Those are all valuable skills, but from my perspective, your daughter needs three additional skills. After working with thousands of children and tweens at camps and schools, here are "Silvana's Three Things Your Daughter Needs to Know."

NUMBER ONE

Your daughter needs to know how to *think creatively*. Businesses complain that employees don't have any new ideas. Managers moan that they can't find employees with innovative thoughts. We hear the phrase, "Think outside the box." I want your daughter to not only think outside the box but also make her own odd-shaped box.

Yes, it's very comfortable and safe to go along with conventional thinking. But where's the fun in being like everyone else? As mothers, we can start helping our daughters to think creatively by setting a good example.

How's this for creativity? (The following situation involves a mother and son, but believe me, the principle applies to mother and daughter also.) A mother grew tired of her son constantly forgetting his lunch. Being the dutiful mother, she delivered the lunch to school so her sweet boy wouldn't go hungry. Each time he'd say, "Thanks, Mom! I promise this is the last time I'll forget." One day, Mom received a phone call from her son, begging for his peanut butter sandwich. Feeling particularly creative, she cheerfully told him his lunch was on the way. Before leaving the house, though, she incorporated her preschool arts and crafts experience. She used a bold red marker to write "Mom loves Jason" all over the bag. She added several yellow happy-face stickers and glued a piece of orange fringe around the top of the bag. A balloon attached to the bag added to the colorful, one-of-a-kind lunch bag. Arriving at the school, she didn't drop the bag off at the office as usual. Oh, no. Mom walked straight into her son's fifth-grade class, smiled at the teacher, and said, "Sorry to interrupt class, Mrs. Myers. I just wanted to give Jason the lunch he forgot." With that, she set the lunch on Jason's desk, placed a kiss on his check, and left the room. That ended the story of "Jason and His Forgotten Lunch."

Some of you might say, "I could never embarrass my daughter like that!" Well, which is better: to nag her all through her school years about forgetting her lunch, or to use creativity to put an end to the situation?

Elizabeth Pace, a marketing and sales expert in Nashville, has also learned to use creativity when dealing with her daughter.

> "I get so frustrated when she rolls her eyes and stomps around and basically acts like a 12-year-old ... even though everything I read says—and other mothers say—this is normal. I carry around a clown's nose (available at any party store for $0.99). When she is being moody, I put it on, no matter if we are driving or at the mall or I may be dropping her off at school. She, of course, is mortified and immediately apologizes and acts nice so that I will not embarrass her in front of her friends."

There you have it, moms. Creativity in the form of a 99-cent clown nose!

A few years ago, we had extra time before seeing a performance of *Annie Get Your Gun* at the Fifth Avenue Theatre in downtown Seattle. Strolling along the street, Sondra shrieked, "Mom! It's a Quicksilver store! I can't believe it! I love Quicksilver." She dashed into the store. I followed, greeted by pulsating music and skimpily dressed headless mannequins. Sondra surveyed the store in the typical 13-year-old way, with a running commentary of "This skirt is darling.... Oh, I love this jacket.... How cool is this sweatshirt!' I tried to maintain an even breathing pattern while looking at the $48 price tags on faded sweatshirts with holes and frayed cuffs.

Sondra, knowing my penchant for being cheap, pulled out all the stops, asking, "Mom, you know I just brought home my report card with a 3.8 GPA. I've been doing my chores without being asked and I babysit for free for kids when you and Dad have a small group at our house. Don't you think you could buy me this sweatshirt?" Naturally her persuasive speech was given with her best "Aren't I the cutest daughter in the world?" dimpled smile. My husband, standing behind me, whispered, "Don't be so cheap. Buy her the ugly, overpriced sweatshirt."

In true motherly fashion, I responded, "Let me think about it." Sondra, in full get-on-Mom's-good-side mode, left the store without protest. This, of course, made me feel even guiltier that my teenager daughter didn't pout or get upset. My plan quickly formed. Since Sondra owned few name-brand clothes, I figured it was time for a treat. While waiting to enter the theater, I shuffled my way into the crowd, out of sight of Allan and Sondra.

I raced back to Quicksilver and told the clerk, "I want to give my daughter a $50 gift certificate, but I don't want her to know it's from me. I have a reputation as a cheap mother to uphold. What can we do to get her the gift certificate when I bring her back here after the show?" The 18-year-old male clerk obviously had never run into this situation in his customer-service training class for Quicksilver. The manager, an "older" woman of maybe 24, overheard my plea and stepped in. "Sure," she said, "let's see what we can do."

I glanced around the store looking for inspiration. Near the store entrance stood a headless mannequin, dressed in only a miniskirt. Her bare chest was actually fairly modest, since a full-size telephone was implanted in her upper torso.

"Does that phone work?" I asked.

The clerk assured me it was an actual phone for free incoming and outgoing calls.

I may be cheap, but I know how to use a half-naked telephone mannequin. "How about this? I'll bring my daughter back and get her to casually be by the phone. You get the phone to ring, because I know she'll answer it. Then maybe ask her a few questions like you are from corporate headquarters. If she answers correctly, direct her to some location in the store where she 'wins' a $50 gift certificate."

Both clerks were obviously amazed at this creative use of their store telephone-chested mannequin. I paid for the gift certificate and made it back to the theater just as the show began.

After the performance, I casually suggested we go back to Quicksilver so Sondra could perhaps find a cheaper item to purchase with her own money. Ever the optimist, Sondra entered the store as I silently pointed and mouthed to the clerk, "That's her."

Sondra strolled through the store, getting closer and closer to the infamous mannequin. Suddenly the phone rang. She looked at me, then at the phone, encased in the chest of a mannequin. No one else was around. The phone kept ringing.

I casually said, "When we were teenagers, we never missed an opportunity to talk to strangers on a payphone."

Sondra cautiously lifted the receiver from the naked chest. "H-e-l-l-o-o," she said.

The rest of the one-sided conversation went like this: "Well, yes, I'm in the store right now.... You want me to tell you the color of the pants in the window? They are red.... The sign above the cash register says 'Yearly Sale.'... Yes, the staff is friendly...." I could see the store manager talking on the phone, bent down behind the main counter so she could peek at Sondra.

Sondra continued answering several questions and then hung up the receiver. With sparkling eyes she said, "That was a call from the corporate headquarters of Quicksilver. They were doing a customer awareness call. I answered all their questions, so they said to go the swimsuit display and look under the stack of flowered suits for a prize!"

She raced over, lifted the suits and saw a coupon for $50. Waving it in the air, she yelled, "I can get that sweatshirt after all!"

Driving home, we had a stimulating conversation about the creative ways mothers dole out money. What this experience teaches you: If you walk by a naked mannequin with a phone in her chest, pick up the receiver when it rings—you never know when you'll be asked to participate in a customer service survey.

Girls growing up in homes where creativity is encouraged soon develop great skills in problem solving. Instead of seeing only one solution for a situation, they see a plethora of possibilities. (Isn't *plethora* a creative word? Try to use *plethora* in a conversation at dinner tonight.)

When Sondra was 11, it rained on Halloween. Not the gentle drizzle that doesn't faze people living in Seattle, but a torrential downpour with winds toppling trees and trick-or-treaters. Lightning added another dangerous element, or she would have still ventured out. Naturally, this canceled Sondra and her friends' plans for going door-to-door loading up on candy. So, that afternoon she came up with a few alternatives:

• Go with her friends to a church-sponsored harvest festival.
• Stay home and eat the candy we bought for trick-or-treaters.
• Have a Halloween carnival in our house.
• Go to Western Washington University, where the college students in the dorms offered candy as kids simply went from room to room.
• Hope the rain stops at the last minute (not likely).

She decided having an indoor carnival in our house would be the most fun. We quickly set up cereal boxes that could be toppled with a beanbag, made an obstacle course in the rec room, and put up a Pin the Tail on the Donkey game. We even had a target on the wall that girls could attempt to hit with a Frisbee. When moms dropped off their daughters, they all told me, "I'm so glad you're doing this. My daughter was so upset she'd have to stay home and do nothing."

That practical experience in creative thinking gave Sondra skills in problem solving, as well as organization as she set up the carnival booths. In 10 years, when she applies for a job as a camp counselor and the interviewer says, "What would you do if it rained on a day you planned to take your campers on a hike?' Sondra will probably reply, "Let me tell you what I did one year when it rained on Halloween..."

Sondra says: Having grown up in my crazy family, I forget that not all families encourage creativity like my parents do. I remember many times when I would have a certain interest for a few weeks. It never lasted long. I'd decide I wanted a horse or that being an actress was cool. For a while, I was fascinated with castles. My parents encouraged my interests, but never spent much money. I had an elaborate set of wooden building blocks that my parents taught me to use. During my horse stage, they bought me a few toy horses at garage sales. Then I spent hours building stalls and barns out of the blocks. When I went through my actress phase, my dad helped me build a stage with the blocks. He added two lights at the end to shine on me when I performed. You wouldn't believe the different castles I built with those blocks! I even remember when my friend Jordan came over in fifth grade. We used the blocks to make a maze for my hamster, Hammy, and timed how long it took him to find some treats. It seemed natural to just creatively use those blocks for whatever interest I had.

So you have two choices: run out and buy your daughter a set of blocks, or incorporate "twisted thinking" into your new creative plan of action. Twisted thinking can help you next the time you wonder, "How can I be creative in this situation?"

Twisted thinkers take an ordinary situation and put a creative "twist" on the situation. Remember when your daughter was in preschool and insisted on dressing herself? You had an adorable outfit selected with red flowered leggings topped with a red sweatshirt embroidered with red hearts. However, your daughter insisted on striped pants and a flowered T-shirt topped with a polka-dotted sundress. When Sondra put her creative wardrobe selections together, I made her a large button that said, "I dressed myself!" She proudly added the button to her ensemble, but every mother understood what it meant.

Try some of these ideas to put a twist on ordinary activities:

- Drive your daughter to school by a different route. Do you notice a new store being built or a house that's painted a strange color?
- Listen to a different radio station for a while. Try classical, country, or a religious station. Discuss the similarities between that station and your regular one.
- If you have a regular church or house of worship, go to another location. For example, if you normally attend a small church, check out a megachurch with parking attendants and even full-size fitness centers.
- Go to the grocery store and put a twist on your regular foods. Buy a fruit you've never tried or check out the imported food aisle.
- The next time your daughter asks, "Can I go over to Jenny's?" respond with "Sure! Just come up with a twisted way of getting there." Let your daughter look for solutions to her everyday situations. Can she carpool with a friend? Is it safe to take a bus? Can she meet Jenny at a halfway point?

Marcella, the mother of a quiet 9-year-old named Heather, showed her daughter a "twisted" way to handle a bully at the bus stop. Mother and daughter packed a wagon full of mini breakfast foods and pulled it to the bus stop. Mom said to the bully, "Hi, Jeff. Marcella talks about you a lot. We thought it would be fun to have a breakfast treat together. Will you help Heather pass out these bagels and apple slices to the other kids while I pour some juice?" Jeff felt special being invited to help with this impromptu celebration. He got attention for being part of the breakfast and from then on stopped picking on Heather. Not every problem disappears with bagels and juice, but it's worth a try!

Great! You and your daughter can now get matching T-shirts that say "We're Twisted Thinkers!" (As Dave Barry would say, "'Twisted Thinkers' sounds like a perfect name for a rock band.")

Mother-Daughter Mini-Activity

Since you're working on "thinking outside the box," here's a way to have a fun time making an origami box. Get a simple origami book at the library or look up one of these sites on the internet so you can make your own box:

- www.kid-at-art.com/htdoc/lesson16.html
- http://glynnorigami.co.uk/Boxes.htm
- http://familycrafts.about.com/od/origami/ (this site even shows you how to make a box out of two one-dollar bills)

Follow the patterns to create your own boxes. See? Not only will your daughter learn to think outside of the box, she can *make* her own box!

Sondra says: Even though at times I think my parents get *too* creative, I do see that creativity pays off. So often, I'll be in school when the teacher asks a question and gets all the typical answers. I'll put a twist on a traditional answer, which teachers love! It's a great way to get good grades without all that extra studying!

NUMBER TWO

The second skill your daughter needs to develop is *resiliency*. We're raising a generation of wimpy girls. I've seen tweens squeal in science class just looking at tadpoles. Only purified water can touch their lip-glossed lips, and they whine at being asked to vacuum the car. Does this conversation take place at your house?

Molly: "I had a horrible day! Don't even talk to me. I'm so stressed out!"
Mom: "What happened?"

Molly: "You'd never understand. You don't know what it's like to be a kid at my school. I just want to go watch TV and forget about my rotten life." (If your daughter is particularly dramatic, she'll tell you about her pathetic, horrendous, unbearable, vile, pitiful life.)

Mom: "Give me a hint about what happened."

Molly: "A hint? I'll give you more than a hint. We're supposed to get a partner and make a display for the science fair. I'm matched up with Sara. She's the biggest geek in school! I can't do it. Now everyone thinks I'm a geek, too. I can't go to school anymore." (Followed by tears and slamming of doors.)

For many girls, the smallest setback turns into: "Oh my Gaaawwwddd! I can't believe this is happening to me. My mom said I can't go bowling until I clean my room. There's too much tension in my life!" High school counselors report girls are stressed out in high school because they don't have decision-making skills. Then colleges tell us freshmen have trouble adjusting to roommates, professors, and getting themselves to class on time. Kids are growing up with all the comforts of a pampered life guided by helicopter parents. This doesn't call for turning your house into a mini military camp, but it does call for helping your daughter learn to be resilient when faced with challenges.

> *Suzanne, mother of a 12-year-old:* "I admit I had a tough childhood. Going to bed hungry was common. I started working—illegally—at a florist at 14. I had to. Otherwise, I wouldn't have had any decent clothes at all, let alone something in fashion. It taught me to be resilient and not let little things get me down. Now, though, I see I'm raising my daughter to get upset over a chipped nail. She'd never be able to handle my childhood."

Many of you know Oprah Winfrey recently spent $40 million to build a girl's leadership academy in South Africa. Tween girls from extremely impoverished backgrounds who displayed strong academic and leadership skills were selected to attend the school. Oprah personally interviewed the final candidates. What she saw in these 11- and 12-year-old girls was resiliency—an inner strength that allowed them to "snap back" from one horrific experience after another. We think our daughters are resilient because they didn't cry when they weren't selected to dance the role of Clara in *The Nutcracker*. Well, one of Oprah's girls shared how she got up at 4:00 AM, walked 20 minutes by herself through one of the toughest shanty villages in South Africa, and then rode the bus for an hour to get to school. Two sisters told Oprah they watched their dad shoot their mother and then turn the gun on himself; they struggle daily for basic food and the chance to go to school. One 11-year-old showed her only school uniform. "I've worn this uniform for six years," she said. "It's very thin and torn in the back."

Yet even in such dire circumstances, these girls displayed a resilient spirit. They helped raise younger siblings, carried heavy buckets of water from a community well, and subsisted on one meal a day. They shared their hopes and dreams with Oprah—to be a teacher, an actress, the president of South Africa.... Instead of rolling their eyes in disgust because they didn't have the latest cell phone, their eyes shone with an inner strength.

Yes, yes, I know you're thinking those girls live in extreme situations and it doesn't apply to your daughter. But actually, it does. If your daughter has life handed to her by her ever-doting mom, she'll never develop the inner strength needed to find her true self.

When Trina was 12, she frequently went with me when my dog Sherman was doing TV commercials. I needed her to help get him to look or move in particular ways. Several directors approached me about using Trina in commercials because they said she was so articulate and outgoing. I resisted, because my goal was to get my dog famous, not my daughter. (Long story in a nutshell: I had a childhood dream to train a dog for TV commercials. Sherman the Wonder Dog ended up with an illustrious career doing commercials for Honda, Chrysler, Reebok, and many others.) I eventually agreed, and Trina soon followed in Sherman's footsteps and filmed numerous commercials and print ads.

While a portion of her earnings went to savings, she did have a bit more spending money than most tweens. Soon she took it for granted that she could earn $75 an hour doing a simple magazine shoot. I wanted her to learn that she was in a special situation most people don't experience. She needed to see how kids her age earned their spending money.

At that time, our rural farming community hired middle school students to pick strawberries in the summer. I quickly signed Trina up for the three-week program, during which a dilapidated bus picked her up at 6:00 AM every day to take her to the berry fields. For the next eight hours, Trina and 200 other kids squatted in the dirt under the hot sun, picking strawberries. On a good day, she'd come home with $4! I wanted her to have an appreciation for people who work in the service industry. She quickly developed resiliency in seeing that it takes effort to get up so early in the summer and do boring physical labor. She picked berries for two summers and I never heard her complain again about having to wait for the camera crew to set up lights during a commercial shoot. She truly gained an understanding for demanding work in trying situations.

Trina picked berries back in the '80s before regulations prohibited kids from working in the fields, so you probably can't sign your daughter up to do that this coming summer. Nevertheless, look for ways to have her "do something hard." Have her spend an hour a day digging a new garden. Get her up at 5:00 AM on a Saturday morning to hand out water at a community marathon. You are not imitating a reform school experience, but she should have experiences that stretch her physically and mentally.

It's one thing to get up early for a dance recital rehearsal where all the attention focuses on your daughter. It's another thing to crawl out of a warm bed and participate in a park cleanup program with *no* emphasis on your daughter. Resiliency comes from meeting challenges that go beyond disappointment at not getting the latest video game.

Sondra says: I attend a school where money isn't really an issue for most kids. They don't have to worry about how they are going to get gas money or be concerned about spending money at upscale restaurants. My parents have raised me to take advantage of free concerts and to buy clothes on sale. It isn't that we don't have the money, it was simply we valued different things. These principles my parents instilled in me really help me keep things in perspective when I go to the mall with my friends. They can easily spend $600 at one store! At times, it's difficult not to get swept up in that spending mentality. My parents could have easily given in and given me the money to go out to eat every night, but they didn't. I must admit I've learned to be resilient when I see my peers with lavish spending styles. My mom and I go to vintage stores, and I get unique clothing pieces no one else has. On the weekends, we go to free art shows, museums, and lectures. I have learned more from those low-cost experiences than I would have from buying the cutest purse or most fashionable sunglasses.

In our house, we simply don't use the phrase, "I'm having a bad day." A "bad day" is when your car dies on the freeway, you're late to work, the boss fires you, and upon returning home, your house burns down—and a fireman trips on his hose and decides to sue you. *That's* a bad day. As a fourth grader, Sondra came home from school once, announcing she had had a bad day. I got out a pencil and paper, and we made a list about her day. The list went like this:

1. Mom woke me up with a backrub
2. Had pancakes for breakfast
3. Got to sit with best friend Amy on bus
4. Teacher let me take lunch count to office (Big time event!)
5. Got an A on spelling test
6. Played with friends at recess
7. Had her favorite sandwich of chicken salad for lunch (So far, this sounds like a pretty good day!)
8. Was leader in walking to music class
9. In music class, Emily said, "You're a horrible singer. I bet you don't make it in the talent show auditions."
10. Got to play basketball in gym
11. Made two free throws and won the game
12. Got to sit with Amy on bus ride home
13. Came home to Mom and a great snack of cantaloupe and crackers

In discussing the list, it was obvious Sondra's "bad day" consisted of 10 bad minutes in music class. We used that technique on several occasions to put a day's events into perspective. There's a big difference between "having a bad day" and "getting irritated in music for 10 minutes." Now she'll come home and, with a smirk, say, "I had an irritating $6\frac{1}{2}$ minutes today. Want to hear about it?"

Dr. Norman Watt, a University of Denver psychologist, defines *resiliency* as "the capacity to respond 'elastically' to life's trials." Resilient people are often described as rubber bands. They stretch and stretch … then bounce back rather than breaking. Studies show that children as young as two years old display traits of resiliency. If a playmate takes her toy, the resilient child doesn't scream or holler. Instead she finds other ways of coping, such as playing with something else or convincing the grabby playmate to give up the toy.

Help your daughter learn some of these skills to increase resiliency:

1. Take control of her life—age-appropriate control, of course! Let her make decisions where logical consequences provide a practical life lesson. Teach your daughter to think of herself as a trailblazer, fearlessly slashing through the jungle with a machete! She's blazing a trail! If everyone at school is complaining about the science project, have her find a way to change the situation. As one mom said, "My daughter was getting upset about a major sixth-grade history project that involved lots of writing. She's more the dramatic type. Laura decided to ask the teacher if she could incorporate all the history facts and do a monologue instead of a report. The teacher agreed, and Laura learned a valuable lesson about taking control." Resilient people take control in an appropriate way.

2. Put the situation in perspective. When faced with adversity, resilient people ask themselves, "How will I feel about this situation in two weeks. In two months? In two years?" Is the situation merely disruptive or life-changing? How do you face adversity? Let's say you were laid off due to corporate downsizing. It's easy to feel discouraged and envision yourself standing on the corner with a "Will Work for Food" sign. On the other hand, after allowing yourself a few days to wallow in self-pity, you can tell yourself, "This is a great opportunity to find a job that is fulfilling as well as financially sound." Then dust off your résumé and start networking toward a new career. In the same way, help your daughter put things in perspective. Try the gnat or mosquito concept. Gnats are tiny insects that annoy us but don't cause swelling and itching like those dreaded mosquitoes. When your daughter faces a challenge, ask her, "Is this a gnat-size problem or a mosquito-size one?" (Not finding her red headband before school is definitely in the gnat category.) If she tells you she's facing a mosquito-size problem, help her out with solutions. If your daughter repeatedly comes home from school crying about her reading ability and the teacher suggests testing her for a learning disability, she's facing a *swarm* of mosquitoes. Helping her differentiate between the two, gives her a realistic appraisal of the situation.

3. Change your mindset about difficult situations. When faced with an adverse condition or obstacle, try asking, "What can I do?" rather than "Why me?" One mother, when told that her newborn had Down Syndrome, kissed her baby and said, "I'm going to become an expert on Down Syndrome so my baby lives the fullest life possible." Now that's resiliency!

4. Give your daughter a chance to s-t-r-e-t-c-h. All too often, we are Super Mom, coming to the rescue for every minor problem. Remember when your daughter was learning to tie her shoes? She'd fumble with the laces, make lopsided bows, and take forever. Didn't you just want to grab her foot and say, "Here, I'll do it for you"? Instead, you watched her struggle, gave her a few words of encouragement, and then heard her proclaim, "I did it myself!" The next time your daughter worries about peer pressure or faces a problem, give her time to s-t-r-e-t-c-h. See if she can work through the situation herself.

Sondra says: There have been many times when my mom has encouraged me to stretch myself. I've been in situations where my mom could easily make a phone call or write a letter and "take care of it." Instead, she encourages me to make the phone call or write the letter to reach my goal. I don't necessarily like it, but I've learned to be resilient and take charge.

NUMBER THREE

Time for the third skill your daughter needs to know. As she gains independence and is away from your watchful eye, your daughter needs a firm grasp of *social skills*. I'm talking about table manners, making eye contact, and speaking in full sentences to adults. Oh, yes, let's not forget to teach our daughters that picking one's nose should be done in private. I've seen girls immediately ostracized at camp if cabin members see her picking her nose. That's the hard fact of tween-girl culture. Girls with an understanding of basic social skills make friends easily and feel competent in various situations. Let's look at some social skills your daughter should master during her tween years, letter by letter.

S: Shake hands with adults when appropriate. No one is asking your daughter to shake hands with classmates on the first day of fifth grade. However, if she meets your boss or a coworker, encourage her to shake hands and introduce herself. Business consultants actually help employees develop a firm handshake. Practice with your daughter so she doesn't give the dreaded "limp fish" handshake.

O: Offer to help. People with social skills are willing to help others. Teach your daughter to volunteer to help with the kindergarten play. If a teacher drops some books, she should pick them up without waiting to see what to do. If she's a guest at someone's house for dinner, she can offer to help set the table.

C: Compliment people. Successful and well-liked people are quick to give compliments. Encourage your daughter to compliment a teacher's new haircut or a student's diorama. A simple "The way you built that log cabin in this shoe-box is so cute!" acknowledges another child's efforts.

I: Introduce yourself and others. Once again, here's your chance to practice your dramatic skills and act out various introductions. How should your daughter introduce her new friend to Grandma? When Trina, our older daughter, was in sixth grade, the teacher practiced introductions with each student. They actually received a grade on how well they introduced parents to the teacher at the first open house.

A: Accept the fact that everyone needs to write thank-you notes. Read any advice column and you'll see many letters complaining about giving a gift for a birthday, graduation, wedding, anniversary, bar mitzvah, or housewarming without getting a thank-you note. Here's the rule: if someone gives your daughter a gift, she sends a thank-you note. (One exception: no need to send a card to her 5-year-old brother who gave her a sculpture made from chewed bubble gum.)

Sondra says: My mother always makes me write thank-you notes. Most times, I ignore them and let them sit on my desk until my mom reminds me that I have to do them. But after sending them, I have gotten so much positive feedback. Most people don't bother to write thank-you notes. By getting your daughter to write them, it puts her one step ahead. You are instilling skills in her that will most definitely help her when she is applying to colleges and scholarships later in life. I know that personally I feel appreciated when I speak somewhere or volunteer and then receive a thank-you note. That simple gesture might be the difference of if I make the extra effort to speak for them in the future. It's a simple courtesy that makes an impact.

L: Lose the "I" in conversation. This is a tough skill for all of us to learn. Have you ever had an adult conversation like this?

You: "Hi, Frances, good to see you. I couldn't make it to book club because my mom was sick."
Frances: "I didn't make it, either. My dog got sick and I had to take him to the vet."
You: "My mom was rushed to the hospital ..."
Frances: "Don't you just hate hospitals? Last time I went to Baptist General, I had to wait two hours in the emergency room."
You: "My mom got admitted right away, but ..."
Frances: "She was lucky. I couldn't get admitted because I lost my insurance card ..."

You want to talk about your mother, and Frances turns every sentence into an excuse to talk about herself. Role-play conversations with your daughter to show her ways to respond to people's conversation. When her friend says, "My mom makes me so mad!" your daughter can ask, "What happened?" rather than, "My mom really upset me last night, too." (Not that you would ever do anything to upset your daughter!)

Mother-Daughter Mini-Activity

The next time you and your daughter are in a casual social setting such as a family party, try not to talk about yourself at all. During any conversation, turn the conversation away from you. Can either one of you go for an hour without saying the word *I*?

S: Speak in full sentences. Tweens have been known to grunt or mumble one-word answers. Let them know this is not acceptable in public or at home with adults. (In our house, a flippant "Whatever" is banned.) If your daughter wants to communicate with her friends with two-word sentences, fine. On the other hand, if a store clerk asks your daughter, "Are you buying this outfit for a special occasion?" she needs to answer with five or more words. A slurred "Cousin's wedding" doesn't count. An appropriate answer is something like, "I'm wearing it to my cousin's wedding next week."

K: Keep elbows off the table. With more and more families eating meals in the car, table manners are becoming a lost art. I read an article that many job interviews now involve the candidate going out to lunch with her potential boss. Employers watch how the candidates treat the wait staff and how they handle table manners. Teaching your daughter to chew with her mouth closed could result in a lucrative job offer! Callie, a 12-year-old, told us, "We hardly ever eat together as a family. I grab something from the refrigerator and eat while watching TV. We had a special award dinner for a science project our class won. I didn't like it. They had all these fancy dishes. I didn't understand why they had two forks by my plate. I didn't know how to act while eating at a table with other people."

I: "I dunno" is a phrase that needs to be wiped from your daughter's vocabulary. Is this a familiar conversation at your house?

"How was your time at Samantha's house?"
"I dunno."
"What would you like for dinner tonight?"
"I dunno."
"Will you be able to get your homework done before dance class?"
"I dunno."

Sounds like you have a not-so-bright daughter. Tweens with social skills know it's polite to answer questions with more than a mumbled "I dunno." She doesn't need to give you a minute-by-minute recap of what happened during the pep rally, but she does owe you a simple answer such as, "The pep band played pretty loud." If your daughter needs help getting the message that "I dunno" is unacceptable, here's a tried-and-true technique. Next time she asks, "Mom will you take Cara and I to the mall?" simply answer, "I dunno."

L: Look for ways to start conversations. Many girls in our surveys said they felt awkward talking to people they don't know. "I met my cousins for the first time," wrote Jenny. "I just stood there and felt like an idiot because I had no idea what to say. It was really awkward." Give your daughter a few opening lines to help begin a two-way conversation. Just saying, "What a cute headband! Where did you get it?" starts a conversation that overcomes a deadly silence.

L: Listen to others. Listening is an all-important social trait many adults lack. We all want to talk, talk, talk, and we disregard that other people might have something to say. It's an old saying, but very true: "We have two ears and one mouth, so we should listen twice as much as we talk." Have a conversation with your daughter in which she makes a conscious effort to listen to you.

S: Share the glory! Did your daughter kick the winning soccer goal? Wonderful! Let her bask in the glory, but also share the credit with other team members. You know how annoying it is at work when one person takes credit for a group project. If your daughter gets the lead in the school play, she should point out how the costumes, lights, and director played a big part in helping her be "the star."

All those tips are basic good manners that apply to all ages. As your daughter demonstrates strong social skills, she will receive positive feedback (especially from other adults), which will reinforce her skills even more.

Many parenting books talk about the need to wash your hands after using the bathroom, wait your turn, and color inside the lines. We know other things are important. So start your daughter on twisted thinking, help her build up resiliency, and work on those social skills!

Just for Fun

Try some twisted thinking in your daughter's bedroom. Give her the opportunity to redecorate her room with creativity rather than a big budget. Can she paint one wall a bright color? How about going to some garage sales and buying a small table, lampshade, or picture frame? Then find ways to embellish those items. Decoupage pictures on top of the table. Add colorful trim around the edge of the lampshade and paint polka dots on the ordinary-looking frame. Your daughter will learn that creativity results in a one-of-a-kind designer bedroom!

Index

About the Authors

SILVANA CLARK is a popular motivational speaker with twenty years experience running enrichment classes, vocational programs, and camp and teen events. Degreed in recreation administration and the mother of three, she has appeared on CNN, QVC, *Home Matters*, *Smart Solutions*, and PAX. She has authored ten earlier books and more than two hundred magazine articles.

SONDRA CLARK is Silvana's seventeen-year-old daughter, an author in her own right, a motivational speaker, as well as the spokesperson for two businesses. Her many awards include the Next Step Super Teen 2007, the Fox TV National Kids Hero Award, the Nestle Very Best in Youth Award and, in 2001 and 2004, The Kids Hall of Fame Award. Sondra has appeared on CNN, Fox, QVC, Discovery Channel, and a total of forty-five televised shows. She has authored eight books.